SONGS FROM THE SOUTHERN SEAS.

SONGS

FROM THE

SOUTHERN SEAS,

And Other Poems.

BY

JOHN BOYLE O'REILLY.

BOSTON:
ROBERTS BROTHERS.
1873.

CAMBRIDGE:
PRESS OF JOHN WILSON AND SON.

TO

CAPTAIN DAVID R. GIFFORD,

OF THE WHALING BARQUE "GAZELLE," OF NEW BEDFORD.

I DEDICATE THIS BOOK.

In February, 1869, I left the coast of Western Australia in a small boat without a sail. Peculiar circumstances rendered it impossible that I should return: my only path lay across the Indian Ocean. It pleased God that my boat was seen from the masthead of the "Gazelle," commanded by Captain GIFFORD, who picked me up and treated me with all kindness during a seven months' whaling cruise. On parting with him at the Cape of Good Hope, he lent me twenty guineas to help me on my way to America. One of the greatest pleasures this little book can ever afford me is the writing of this dedication.

PREFACE.

It may be well to say in the opening of this book that many of the scenes therein shown are taken from a land blessed by God and blighted by man, — a Penal Colony. Western Australia, the poorest and the loveliest of all the Australias, has received from the mother country only her shame and her crime.

I cannot write excuses for the many faults and crudities in this first book: if nobody else can prize the volume, I myself can. Not for its literary worth, indeed; but for many hours of pleasure which its composition has given to me. Whatever merit it may be denied, it must certainly possess that, if merit it be, of realism. Many of the scenes shown are memories, not imaginings, — things which clamored for recognition, and I have written them here.

THE AUTHOR.

CONTENTS.

Delightful land, in wildness even benign,
The glorious past is ours, the future thine!
As in a cradled Hercules, we trace
The lines of empire in thine infant face.
What nations in thy wide horizon's span
Shall teem on tracts untrodden yet by man!
What spacious cities with their spires shall gleam
Where now the panther laps a lonely stream,
And all but brute or reptile life is dumb!
Land of the free! thy kingdom is to come.

Campbell.

Nor gold nor silver are the words set here,
Nor rich-wrought chasing on design of art;
But rugged relics of an unknown sphere
Where fortune chanced I played one time a part.
I say not this to pity move, or praise,—
This little, faulty book is all my own,
In which I've writ of men and things and ways
Uncouth and rough as Austral ironstone.

It may be, I have left the higher gleams
Of skies and flowers unheeded or forgot;
It may be so,—but, looking back, it seems
When I was with them I beheld them not.
I was no rambling poet, but a man
Hard-pressed to dig and delve, with naught of ease
The hot day through, save when the evening's fan
Of sea-winds rustled through the kindly trees.

It may be so; but when I think I smile
At my poor hand and brain to paint the charms
Of God's first-blazoned canvas! here the aisle
Moonlit and deep of reaching gothic arms

From towering gums, mahogany, and palm,
And odorous jam and sandal; there the growth
Of arm-long velvet leaves grown hoar in calm, —
In calm unbroken since their luscious youth.

How can I show you all the silent birds
With strange metallic glintings on the wing?
Or how tell half their sadness in cold words, —
The poor dumb lutes, the birds that never sing?
Of wondrous parrot-greens and iris hue
Of sensuous flower and of gleaming snake, —
Ah! what I see I long that so might you,
But of these things what picture can I make?

Sometime, maybe, a man will wander there, —
A mind God-gifted, and not dull and weak;
And he will come and paint that land so fair,
And show the beauties of which I but speak.
But in the hard, sad days that there I spent,
My mind absorbed rude pictures: these I show
As best I may, and just with this intent, —
To tell some things that all folk may not know.

WESTERN AUSTRALIA.

THE KING OF THE VASSE.

A LEGEND OF THE BUSH.

From that fair land and drear land in the South,
Of which through years I do not cease to think,
I brought a tale, learned not by word of mouth,
But formed by finding here one golden link
And there another; and with hands unskilled
For such fine work, but patient of all pain
For love of it, I sought therefrom to build
What might have been at first the goodly chain.

It is not golden now: my craft knows more
Of working baser metal than of fine;
But to those fate-wrought rings of precious ore
I add these rugged iron links of mine.

SONGS FROM THE SOUTHERN SEAS.

THE KING OF THE VASSE.

A LEGEND OF THE BUSH.

MY tale which I have brought is of a time
Ere that fair Southern land was stained with crime,
Brought thitherward in reeking ships and cast
Like blight upon the coast, or like a blast
From angry levin on a fair young tree,
That stands thenceforth a piteous sight to see.
So stands this land to-day beneath the sun,—
A weltering plague-spot; while not any one
Of all the Christian lands upon the earth,
Not e'en the rock that last had ocean birth,
Would call her sister,—she, the fairest shore
In all the Southern Ocean o'er and o'er.
Poor Cinderella! she must weep her woe,
Because an elder sister wills it so.

Ah! could that sister see the future day
When her own wealth and strength are shorn
  away,
And she, lone mother then, puts forth her hand
To rest on kindred blood in that far land;
Could she but see that kin deny her claim
Because of nothing owing her but shame, —
Then might she learn 'tis building but to fall,
If carted rubble be the basement-wall.

But this my tale, if tale it be, begins
Before the young land saw the old land's sins
Sail up the orient ocean, like a cloud
Far-blown, and widening as it neared, — a shroud
Fate-sent to wrap the bier of all things pure,
And mark the leper-land while stains endure.

In the far days, the few who sought the West
Were men all guileless, in adventurous quest
Of lands to feed their flocks and raise their grain,
And help them live their lives with less of pain
Than crowded Europe lets her children know.

From their old homesteads did they seaward go,
As if in Nature's order men must flee
As flow the streams,—from inlands to the sea.

In that far time, from out a Northern land,
With home-ties severed, went a numerous band
Of men and wives and children, white-haired folk:
Whose humble hope of rest at home had broke,
As year was piled on year, and still their toil
Had wrung poor fee from Sweden's rugged soil.
One day there gathered from the neighboring steads,
In Jacob Eibsen's, five strong household heads,—
Five men large-limbed and sinewed, Jacob's sons,
Though he was hale, as one whose current runs
In stony channels, that the streamlet rend,
But keep it clear and full unto the end.
Eight sons had Jacob Eibsen,—three still boys,
And these five men, who owned of griefs and joys
The common lot; and three tall girls beside,
Of whom the eldest was a blushing bride

One year before. Old-fashioned times and men,
And wives and maidens, were in Sweden then.
These five came there for counsel: they were
tired
Of hoping on for all the heart desired;
And Jacob, old but mighty-thewed as youth,
In all their words did sadly own the truth,
And said unto them, "Wealth cannot be found
In Sweden now by men who till the ground.
I've thought at times of leaving this bare place,
And holding seaward with a seeking face
For those new lands they speak of, where men
thrive.
Alone I've thought of this; but now you five —
Five brother men of Eibsen blood — shall say
If our old stock from here must wend their
way,
And seek a home where anxious sires can give
To every child enough whereon to live."

Then each took thought in silence. Jacob gazed
Across them at the pastures worn and grazed

By ill-fed herds; his glance to corn-fields passed,
Where stunted oats, worse each year than the last,
And blighted barley, grew amongst the stones,
That showed ungainly, like earth's fleshless bones.
He sighed, and turned away. "Sons, let me know
What think you."

Each one answered firm, "We go."
And then they said, "We want no northern wind
To chill us more, or driving hail to blind.
But let us sail where south winds fan the sea,
And happier we and all our race shall be."
And so in time there started for the coast,
With farm and household gear, this Eibsen host;
And there, with others, to a good ship passed,
Which soon of Sweden's hills beheld the last.

I know not of their voyage, nor how they
Did wonder-stricken sit, as day by day,
'Neath tropic rays, they saw the smooth sea swell
And heave; while night by night the north-star
fell,

Till last they watched him burning on the sea;
Nor how they saw, and wondered it could be,
Strange beacons rise before them as they gazed;
Nor how their hearts grew light when southward blazed
Five stars in blessed shape, — the Cross! whose flame
Seemed shining welcome as the wanderers came.

My story presses from this star-born hope
To where on young New Holland's western slope
These Northern farming folk found homes at last,
And all their thankless toil seemed now long past.

Nine fruitful years chased over, and nigh all
Of life was sweet. But one dark drop of gall
Had come when first they landed, like a sign
Of some black woe; and deep in Eibsen's wine
Of life it hid, till in the sweetest cup
The old man saw its shape come shuddering up.

And first it came in this wise: when their ship
Had made the promised land, and every lip
Was pouring praise for what the eye did meet,—
For all the air was yellow as with heat
Above the peaceful sea and dazzling sand
That wooed each other round the beauteous land,
Where inward stretched the slumbering forest's
green,—
When first these sights from off the deck were
seen,
There rose a wailing sternwards, and the men
Who dreamt of heaven turned to earth agen,
And heard the direful cause with bated breath,—
The land's first gleam had brought the blight of
death!

The wife of Eibsen held her six-years son,
Her youngest, and in secret best-loved one,
Close to her lifeless: his had been the cry
That first horizonwards bent every eye;
And from that opening sight of sand and tree
Like one deep spell-bound did he seem to be,

And moved by some strange phantasy; his eyes
Were wide distended as in glad surprise
At something there he saw; his arms reached
o'er
The vessel's side as if to greet the shore,
And sounds came from his lips like sobs of joy.

A brief time so; and then the blue-eyed boy
Sank down convulsed, as if to him appeared
Strange sights that they saw not; and all afeard
Grew the late joyous people with vague dread;
And loud the mother wailed above her dead.

The ship steered in and found a bay, and then
The anchor plunged aweary-like: the men
Breathed breaths of rest at treading land agen.

Upon the beach by Christian men untrod
The wanderers kneeling offered up to God
The land's first-fruits; and nigh the kneeling band
The burdened mother sat upon the sand,
And still she wailed, not praying.

'Neath the wood
That lined the beach a crowd of watchers stood:
Tall men spear-armed, with skins like dusky night,
And aspect blended of deep awe and fright.
The ship that morn they saw, like some vast bird,
Come sailing toward their country; and they heard
The voices now of those strange men whose eyes
Were turned aloft, who spake unto the skies!

They heard and feared, not knowing, that first
prayer,
But feared not when the wail arose, for there
Was some familiar thing did not appall,—
Grief, common heritage and lot of all.
They moved and breathed more freely at the cry,
And slowly from the wood, and timorously,
They one by one emerged upon the beach.
The white men saw, and like to friends did reach
Their hands unarmed; and soon the dusky crowd
Drew nigh and stood where wailed the mother
loud.
They claimed her kindred, they could understand

That woe was hers and theirs; whereas the band
Of white-skinned men did not as brethren seem.

But now, behold! a man, whom one would deem
From eye and mien, wherever met, a King,
Did stand beside the woman. No youth's spring
Was in the foot that naked pressed the sand;
No warrior's might was in the long dark hand
That waved his people backward; no bright gold
Of lace or armor glittered; gaunt and old, —
A belt, half apron, made of emu-down,
Upon his loins; upon his head no crown
Save only that which eighty years did trace
In whitened hair above his furrowed face.
Nigh nude he was: a short fur boka hung
In toga-folds upon his back, but flung
From his right arm and shoulder, — ever there
The spear-arm of the warrior is bare.

So stood he nigh the woman, gaunt and wild
But king-like, spearless, looking on the child
That lay with livid face upon her knees.

Thus long and fixed he gazed, as one who sees
A symbol hidden in a simple thing,
And trembles at its meaning: so the King
Fell trembling there, and from his breast there
broke
A cry, part joy, part fear; then to his folk
With upraised hands he spoke one guttural word,
And said it over thrice; and when they heard,
They, too, were stricken with strange fear and joy.

The white-haired King then to the breathless boy
Drew closer still, while all the dusky crowd
In weird abasement to the earth were bowed.
Across his breast the aged ruler wore
A leathern thong or belt; whate'er it bore
Was hidden 'neath the boka. As he drew
Anigh the mother, from his side he threw
Far back the skin that made his rich-furred robe,
And showed upon the belt a small red globe
Of carven wood, bright-polished, as with years:
When this they saw, deep grew his people's fears,
And to the white sand were their foreheads
pressed.

The King then raised his arms, as if he blest
The youth who lay there seeming dead and cold;
Then took the globe and oped it, and behold!
Within it, bedded in the carven case,
There lay a precious thing for that rude race
To hold, though it as God they seemed to prize,—
A Pearl of purest hue and wondrous size!

And as the sunbeams kissed it, from the dead
The dusk King looked, and o'er his snowy head
With both long hands he raised the enthroned
gem,
And turned him toward the strangers: e'en on
them
Before the lovely Thing, an awe did fall
To see that worship deep and mystical,
That King with upraised god, like rev'rent priest
With elevated Host at Christian feast.

Then to the mother turning slow, the King
Took out the Pearl, and laid the beauteous Thing
Upon the dead boy's mouth and brow and breast,

And as it touched him, lo! the awful rest
Of death was broken, and the youth uprose!

. . . . . .

Nine years passed over since on that fair shore
The wanderers knelt,—but wanderers they no
more.
With hopeful hearts they bore the promise-pain
Of early labor, and soon bending grain
And herds and homesteads and a teeming soil
A thousand-fold repaid their patient toil.

Nine times the sun's high glory glared above,
As if his might set naught on human love,
But yearned to scorn and scorch the things that
grew
On man's poor home, till all the forest's hue
Of blessed green was burned to dusty brown;
And still the ruthless rays rained fiercely down,
Till insects, reptiles, shrivelled as they lay,
And piteous cracks, like lips, in parching clay
Sent silent pleadings skyward,—as if she,

The fruitful, generous mother, plaintively
Did wail for water. Lo! her cry is heard,
And swift, obedient to the Ruler's word,
From Southern iceland sweeps the cool sea breeze,
To fan the earth and bless the suffering trees,
And bear dense clouds with bursting weight of
rain
To soothe with moisture all the parching pain.

Oh, Mercy's sweetest symbol! only they
Who see the earth agape in burning day,
Who watch its living things thirst-stricken lie,
And turn from brazen heaven as they die, —
Their hearts alone, the shadowy cloud can prize
That veils the sun, — as to poor earth-dimmed eyes
The sorrow comes to veil our joy's dear face,
All rich in mercy and in God's sweet grace!

Thrice welcome, clouds from seaward, settling down
O'er thirsting nature! Now the trees' dull brown
Is washed away, and leaflet buds appear,
And youngling undergrowth, and far and near

The bush is whispering in her pent-up glee,
As myriad roots bestir them to be free,
And drink the soaking moisture; while bright
 heaven
Shows clear, as inland are the spent clouds driven;
And oh! that arch, that sky's intensest hue!
That deep, God-painted, unimagined blue.
Through which the golden sun now smiling sails,
And sends his love to fructify the vales
That late he seemed to curse! Earth throbs and
 heaves
With pregnant prescience of life and leaves;
The shadows darken 'neath the tall trees' screen,
While round their stems the rank and velvet green
Of undergrowth is deeper still; and there,
Within the double shade and steaming air,
The scarlet palm has fixed its noxious root,
And hangs the glorious poison of its fruit;
And there, 'mid shaded green and shaded light,
The steel-blue silent birds take rapid flight
From earth to tree and tree to earth; and there
The crimson-plumaged parrot cleaves the air

Like flying fire, and huge brown owls awake
To watch, far down, the stealing carpet snake,
Fresh-skinned and glowing in his changing dyes,
With evil wisdom in the cruel eyes
That glint like gems as o'er his head flits by
The blue-black armor of the emperor-fly;
And all the humid earth displays its powers
Of prayer, with incense from the hearts of flowers
That load the air with beauty and with wine
Of mingled color, as with one design
Of making there a carpet to be trod,
In woven splendor, by the feet of God!

And high o'erhead is color: round and round
The towering gums and tuads, closely wound
Like cables, creep the climbers to the sun,
And over all the reaching branches run
And hang, and still send shoots that climb and wind
Till every arm and spray and leaf is twined,
And miles of trees, like brethren joined in love,
Are drawn and laced; while round them and above,

When all is knit, the creeper rests for days
As gathering might, and then one blinding blaze
Of very glory sends, in wealth and strength,
Of scarlet flowers o'er the forest's length!

Such scenes as these have subtile power to trace
Their clear-lined impress on the mind and face;
And these strange simple folk, not knowing why,
Grew more and more to silence; and the eye,
The quiet eye of Swedish gray, grew deep
With listening to the solemn rustling sweep
From wings of Silence, and the earth's great psalm
Intoned forever by the forest's calm.

But most of all was younger Jacob changed:
From morn till night, alone, the woods he ranged,
To kindred, pastime, sympathy estranged.
Since that first day of landing from the ship
When with the Pearl on brow and breast and lip
The aged King had touched him and he rose;
His former life had left him, and he chose
The woods as home, the wild, uncultured men
As friends and comrades. It were better then,

His brethren said, the boy had truly died
Than they should live to be by him denied,
As now they were. He lived in sombre mood,
He spoke no word to them, he broke no food
That they did eat: his former life was dead, —
The soul brought back was not the soul that
 fled!
'Twas Jacob's form and feature, but the light
Within his eyes was strange unto their sight.

His mother's grief was piteous to see:
Unloving was he to the rest, but she
Held undespairing hope that deep within
Her son's changed heart was love that she might
 win
By patient tenderness; and so she strove
For nine long years, but won no look of love!

At last his brethren gazed on him with awe,
And knew untold that from the form they saw
Their brother's gentle mind was sure dispelled,
And now a gloomy savage soul it held.

From that first day, close intercourse he had
With those who raised him up,—fierce men, unclad,
Spear-armed and wild, in all their ways uncouth,
And strange to every habit of his youth.
His food they brought, his will they seemed to crave,
The wildest bushman tended like a slave;
He worked their charms, their hideous chants he sung;
Though dumb to all his own, their guttural tongue
He often spoke in tones of curt command,
And kinged it proudly o'er the dusky band.

And once each year there gathered from afar
A swarming host, as if a sudden war
Had called them forth, and with them did they bring
In solemn, savage pomp the white-haired King,
Who year by year more withered was and weak;
And he would lead the youth apart and speak

Some occult words, and from the carven case
Would take the Pearl and touch the young man's
face,
And hold it o'er him blessing; while the crowd,
As on the shore, in dumb abasement bowed.
And when the King had closed the formal rite,
The rest held savage revelry by night,
Round blazing fires, with dance and orgies base,
That roused the sleeping echoes of the place,
Which down the forest vistas moaned the din,
Like spirits pure beholding impious sin.

Nine times they gathered thus; but on the last
The old king's waning life seemed well-nigh past.
His feeble strength had failed: he walked no
more,
But on a woven spear-wood couch they bore
With careful tread the form that barely gasped,
As if the door of death now hung unhasped,
Awaiting but a breath to swing, and show
The dim eternal plain that stretched below.

The tenth year waned: the cloistered bush was
stilled,
The earth lay sleeping, while the clouds distilled
In ghostly veil their blessing. Thin and white,
Through opening trees the moonbeams cleft the
night,
And showed the sombre arches, taller far
Than grandest aisles of built cathedrals are.
And up those dim-lit aisles in silence streamed
Tall men with trailing spears, until it seemed,
So many lines converged of endless length,
A nation there was gathered in its strength.

Around one spot was kept a spacious ring,
Where lay the body of the white-haired King,
Which all the spearmen gathered to behold
Upon its spear-wood litter, stiff and cold.
All naked, there the dusky corse was laid
Beneath a royal tuad's mourning shade;
Upon the breast was placed the carven case
That held the symbol of their ancient race,

And eyes awe-stricken saw the mystic Thing
That soon would clothe another as their King!
The midnight moon was high and white o'erhead,
And threw a ghastly pallor round the dead
That heightened still the savage pomp and state
In which they stood expectant, as for Fate
To move and mark with undisputed hand
The one amongst them to the high command.
And long they stood unanswered; each on each
Had looked in vain for motion or for speech:
Unmoved as ebon statues, grand and tall,
They ringed the shadowy circle, silent all.

Then came a creeping tremor, as a breeze
With cooling rustle moves the summer trees
Before the thunder crashes on the ear;
The dense ranks turn expectant, as they hear
A sound, at first afar, but nearing fast;
The outer crowd divides, as waves are cast
On either side a tall ship's cleaving bow,
Or mould is parted by the fearless plough
That leaves behind a passage clear and broad:

So through the murmuring multitude a road
Was cleft with power, up which in haughty swing
A figure stalking broke the sacred ring,
And stood beside the body of the King!

'Twas Jacob Eibsen, sad and gloomy-browed,
Who bared his neck and breast, one moment bowed
Above the corse, and then stood proud and tall,
And held the carven case before them all!
A breath went upward like a smothered fright
From every heart, to see that face, so white,
So foreign to their own, but marked with might
From source unquestioned, and to them divine;
Whilst he, the master of the mystic sign,
Then oped the case and took the Pearl and raised,
As erst the King had done, and upward gazed,
As swearing fealty to God on high!

But ere the oath took form, there thrilled a cry
Of shivering horror through the hush of night;
And there before him, blinded by the sight

Of all his impious purpose, brave with love,
His mother stood, and stretched her arms above
To tear the idol from her darling's hand ;
But one fierce look, and rang a harsh command
In Jacob's voice, that smote her like a sword.
A thousand men sprang forward at the word,
To tear the mother from the form of stone,
And cast her forth ; but, as he stood alone,
The keen, heart-broken wail that cut the air
Went two-edged through him, half reproach, half
prayer.

But all unheeding, he nor marked her cry
By sign or look within the gloomy eye ;
But round his body bound the carven case,
And swore the fealty with marble face.

As fades a dream before slow-waking sense,
The shadowy host, that late stood fixed and dense,
Began to melt ; and as they came erewhile,
The streams flowed backward through each moon-
lit aisle ;

And soon he stood alone within the place,
Their new-made king, — their king with pallid face,
Their king with strange foreboding and unrest,
And half-formed thoughts, like dreams, within his
breast.
Like Moses' rod, that mother's cry of woe
Had struck for water; but the fitful flow
That weakly welled and streamed did seem to
mock
Before it died forever on the rock.

The sun rose o'er the forest, and his light
Made still more dreamlike all the evil night.
Day streamed his glory down the aisles' dim arch,
All hushed and shadowy like a pillared church;
And through the lonely bush no living thing
Was seen, save now and then a garish wing
Of bird low-flying on its silent way.

But woful searchers spent the weary day
In anxious dread, and found not what they
sought, —

Their mother and their brother: evening brought
A son and father to the lonesome place
That saw the last night's scene; and there, her face
Laid earthward, speaking dumbly to her heart,
They found her, as the hands that tore apart
The son and mother flung her from their chief,
And with one cry her heart had spent its grief.

They bore the cold earth that so late did move
In household happiness and works of love,
Unto their rude home, lonely now; and he
Who laid her there, from present misery
Did turn away, half-blinded by his tears,
To see with inward eye the far-off years
When Swedish toil was light and hedgerows sweet;
Where, when the toil was o'er, he used to meet
A simple gray-eyed girl, with sun-browned face,
Whose love had won his heart, and whose sweet grace
Had blessed for threescore years his humble life.

So Jacob Eibsen mourned his faithful wife,
And found the world no home when she was gone.
The days that seemed of old to hurry on
Now dragged their course, and marred the wish
    that grew,
When first he saw her grave, to sleep there too.
But though to him, whose yearning hope outran
The steady motion of the seasons' plan,
The years were slow in coming, still their pace
With awful sureness left a solemn trace,
Like dust that settles on an open page,
On Jacob Eibsen's head, bent down with age;
And ere twice more the soothing rains had come,
The old man had his wish, and to his home,
Beneath the strange trees' shadow where she lay,
They bore the rude-made bier; and from that day,
When round the parent graves the brethren stood,
Their new-made homesteads were no longer good,
But marked they seemed by some o'erhanging
    dread
That linked the living with the dreamless dead.

Grown silent with the woods the men were all,
But words were needed not to note the pall
That each one knew hung o'er them. Duties now,
With straying herds or swinging scythe, or plough,
Were cheerless tasks: like men they were who wrought
A weary toil that no repayment brought.
And when the seasons came and went, and still
The pall was hanging o'er them, with one will
They yoked their oxen teams and piled the loads
Of gear selected for the aimless roads
That nature opens through the bush; and when
The train was ready, women-folk and men
Went over to the graves and wept and prayed,
Then rose and turned away, but still delayed
Ere leaving there forever those poor mounds.

The next bright sunrise heard the teamsters' sounds
Of voice and whip a long day's march away;
And wider still the space grew day by day

From their old resting-place: the trackless wood
Still led them on with promises of good,
As when the mirage leads a thirsty band
With palm-tree visions o'er the arid sand.

I know not where they settled down at last:
Their lives and homes from out my tale have passed,
And left me naught, or seeming naught, to trace
But cheerless record of the empty place,
Where long unseen the palm-thatched cabins stood,
And made more lonely still the lonesome wood.

Long lives of men passed over; but the years,
That line men's faces with hard cares and tears,
Pass lightly o'er a forest, leaving there
No wreck of young disease or old despair;
For trees are mightier than men, and Time,
When left by cunning Sin and dark-browed Crime
To work alone, hath ever gentle mood.
Unchanged the pillars and the arches stood,

But shadowed taller vistas ; and the earth,
That takes and gives the ceaseless death and birth,
Was blooming still, as once it bloomed before
When sea-tired eyes beheld the beauteous shore.

But man's best work is weak, nor stands nor
grows
Like Nature's simplest. Every breeze that blows,
Health-bearing to the forest, plays its part
In hasting graveward all his humble art.

Beneath the trees the cabins still remained,
By all the changing seasons seared and stained ;
Grown old and weirdlike, as the folk might grow
In such a place, who left them long ago.

Men came, and wondering found the work of
men
Where they had deemed them first. The savage
then
Heard through the wood the axe's deathwatch
stroke
For him and all his people : odorous smoke

Of burning sandal rose where white men dwelt,
Around the huts ; but they had shuddering felt
The weird, forbidden aspect of the spot,
And left the place untouched to mould and rot.
The woods grew blithe with labor : all around,
From point to point, was heard the hollow sound,
The solemn, far-off clicking on the ear
That marks the presence of the pioneer.
And children came like flowers to bless the toil
That reaped rich fruitage from the virgin soil ;
And through the woods they wandered fresh and fair,
To feast on all the beauties blooming there.
But always did they shun the spot where grew,
From earth once tilled, the flowers of rarest hue.
There wheat grown wild in rank luxuriance spread,
And fruits grown native ; but a sudden tread
Or bramble's fall would foul goanos wake,
Or start the chilling rustle of the snake ;
And diamond eyes of these and thousand more,
Gleamed out from ruined roof and wall and floor.

The new-come people, they whose axes rung
Throughout the forest, spoke the English tongue,
And never knew that men of other race
From Europe's fields had settled in the place ;
But deemed these huts were built some long-past
day
By lonely seamen who were cast away
And thrown upon the coast, who there had built
Their homes, and lived until some woe or guilt
Was bred among them, and they fled the sight
Of scenes that held a horror to the light.

But while they thought such things, the spell that
hung,
And cast its shadow o'er the place, was strung
To utmost tension that a breath would break,
And show between the rifts the deep blue lake
Of blessed peace, — as next to sorrow lies
A stretch of rest, rewarding hopeful eyes.
And while such things bethought this new-come
folk,
That breath was breathed, the olden spell was
broke :

From far away within the unknown land,
O'er belts of forest and o'er wastes of sand,
A cry came thrilling, like a cry of pain
From suffering heart and half-awakened brain ;
As one thought dead who wakes within the tomb,
And, reaching, cries for sunshine in the gloom.

In that strange country's heart, whence comes the
breath
Of hot disease and pestilential death,
Lie leagues of wooded swamp, that from the hills
Seem stretching meadows ; but the flood that fills
Those valley-basins has the hue of ink,
And dismal doorways open on the brink,
Beneath the gnarlèd arms of trees that grow
All leafless to the top, from roots below
The Lethe flood ; and he who enters there
Beneath their screen sees rising, ghastly-bare,
Like mammoth bones within a charnel dark,
The white and ragged stems of paper-bark,
That drip down moisture with a ceaseless drip,
From lines that run like cordage of a ship ;

For myriad creepers struggle to the light,
And twine and mat o'erhead in murderous
fight
For life and sunshine, like another race
That wars on brethren for the highest place.
Between the water and the matted screen,
The baldhead vultures, two and two, are seen
In dismal grandeur, with revolting face
Of foul grotesque, like spirits of the place;
And now and then a spear-shaped wave goes by,
Its apex glittering with an evil eye
That sets above its enemy and prey,
As from the wave in treacherous, slimy way
The black snake winds, and strikes the bestial bird,
Whose shriek-like wailing on the hills is heard.

Beyond this circling swamp, a circling waste
Of baked and barren desert land is placed,—
A land of awful grayness, wild and stark,
Where man will never leave a deeper mark,
On leagues of fissured clay and scorching stones,
Than may be printed there by bleaching bones.

Within this belt, that keeps a savage guard,
As round a treasure sleeps a dragon ward,
A forest stretches far of precious trees;
Whence came, one day, an odor-laden breeze
Of jam-wood bruised, and sandal sweet in smoke.
For there long dwelt a numerous native folk
In that heart-garden of the continent, —
There human lives with aims and fears were spent,
And marked by love and hate and peace and pain,
And hearts well-filled and hearts athirst for gain,
And lips that clung, and faces bowed in shame;
For, wild or polished, man is still the same,
And loves and hates and envies in the wood,
With spear and boka and with manners rude,
As loves and hates his brother shorn and sleek,
Who learns by lifelong practice how to speak
With oily tongue, while in his heart below
Lies rankling poison that he dare not show.

Afar from all new ways this people dwelt,
And knew no books, and to no God had knelt,

And had no codes to rule them writ in blood;
But savage, selfish, nomad-lived and rude,
With human passions fierce from unrestraint,
And free as their loose limbs; with every taint
That earth can give to that which God has given;
Their nearest glimpse of Him, o'er-arching heaven,
Where dwelt the giver and preserver, — Light,
Who daily slew and still was slain by Night.

A savage people they, and prone to strife;
Yet men grown weak with years had spent a life
Of peace unbroken, and their sires, long dead,
Had equal lives of peace unbroken led.
It was no statute's bond or coward fear
Of retribution kept the shivering spear
In all those years from fratricidal sheath;
But one it was who ruled them, — one whom Death
Had passed as if he saw not, — one whose word
Through all that lovely central land was heard
And bowed to, as of yore the people bent,
In desert wanderings, to a leader sent

To guide and guard them to a promised land.
O'er all the Austral tribes he held command, —
A man unlike them and not of their race,
A man of flowing hair and pallid face,
A man who strove by no deft juggler's art
To keep his kingdom in the people's heart,
Nor held his place by feats of brutal might
Or showy skill, to please the savage sight;
But one who ruled them as a King of kings,
A man above, not of them, — one who brings,
To prove his kingship to the low and high,
The inborn power of the regal eye!

Like him of Sinai with the stones of law,
Whose people almost worshipped when they saw
The veilèd face whereon God's glory burned;
But yet who, mutable as water, turned
From that veiled ruler who had talked with God,
To make themselves an idol from a clod:
So turned one day this savage Austral race
Against their monarch with the pallid face.
The young men knew him not, the old had heard
In far-off days, from men grown old, a word

That dimly lighted up the mystic choice
Of this their alien King, — how once a voice
Was heard by their own monarch calling clear,
And leading onward, where as on a bier
A dead child lay upon a woman's knees ;
Whom when the old King saw, like one who sees
Far through the mist of common life, he spoke
And touched him with the Pearl, and he awoke,
And from that day the people owned his right
To wear the Pearl and rule them, when the light
Had left their old King's eyes. But now, they said,
The men who owned that right were too long dead;
And they were young and strong and held their spears
In idle resting through this white King's fears,
Who still would live to rule them till they changed
Their men to puling women, and estranged
To Austral hands the spear and coila grew.

And so they rose against him, and they slew
The white-haired men who raised their hands to warn,

And true to ancient trust in warning fell,
While o'er them rang the fierce revolters' yell.
Then midst the dead uprose the King in scorn,
Like some strong, hunted thing that stands at
bay
To win a brief but desperate delay.
A moment thus, and those within the ring
'Gan backward press from their unarmèd King,
Who swept his hand as though he bade them fly,
And brave no more the anger of his eye.
The heaving crowd grew still before that face,
And watched him take the ancient carven case,
And ope it there, and take the Pearl and stand
As once before he stood, with upraised hand
And upturned eyes of inward worshipping.

Awe-struck and dumb, once more they owned him
King,
And humbly crouched before him; when a sound,
A whirring sound that thrilled them, passed o'er-
head,
And with a spring they rose: a spear had sped

With aim unerring and with deathful might,
And split the awful centre of their sight, —
The upraised Pearl! A moment there it shone
Before the spear-point, — then forever gone!

° ° ° ° °

The spell that long the ruined huts did shroud
Was rent and scattered, as a hanging cloud
In moveless air is torn and blown away
By sudden gust uprising; and one day
When evening's lengthened shadows came to hush
The children's voices, and the awful bush
Was lapt in sombre stillness, and on high
Above the arches stretched the frescoed sky, —
When all the scene such chilling aspect wore
As marked one other night long years before,
When through the reaching trees the moonlight
shone
Upon a prostrate form, and o'er it one
With kingly gesture. Now the light is shed
No more on youthful brow and daring head,

But on a man grown weirdly old, whose face
Keeps turning ever to some new-found place
That rises up before him like a dream ;
And not unlike a dreamer does he seem,
Who might have slept, unheeding time's sure flow,
And woke to find a world he does not know.
His long white hair flows o'er a form low bowed
By wondrous weight of years : he speaks aloud
In garbled Swedish words, with piteous wist,
As long-lost objects rise through memory's mist.
Again and once again his pace he stays,
As crowding images of other days
Loom up before him dimly, and he sees
A vague, forgotten friendship in the trees
That reach their arms in welcome ; but agen
These olden glimpses vanish, and dark men
Are round him, dumb and crouching, and he stands
With guttural sentences and upraised hands,
That hold a carven case, — but empty now,
Which makes more pitiful the aged brow

Full-turned to those tall tuads that did hear
A son's fierce mandate and a mother's prayer.

Ah, God! what memories can live of these,
Save only with the half-immortal trees
That saw the death of one, the other lost?

The weird-like figure now the bush has crost
And stands within the ring, and turns and moans,
With arms out-reaching and heart-piercing tones,
And groping hands, as one a long time blind
Who sees a glimmering light on eye and mind.
From tree to sky he turns, from sky to earth,
And gasps as one to whom a second birth
Of wondrous meaning is an instant shown.

Who is this wreck of years, who all alone,
In savage raiment and with words unknown,
Bows down like some poor penitent who fears
The wrath of God provoked?—this man who hears
Around him now, wide circling through the wood
The breathing stillness of a multitude?

Who catches dimly through his straining sight
The misty vision of an impious rite?
Who hears from one a cry that rends his heart,
And feels that loving arms are torn apart,
And by his mandate fiercely thrust aside?
Who is this one who crouches where she died,
With face laid earthward as her face was laid,
And prays for her as she for him once prayed?

'Tis Jacob Eibsen, Jacob Eibsen's son,
Whose occult life and mystic rule are done,
And passed away the memory from his brain.
'Tis Jacob Eibsen, who has come again
To roam the woods, and see the mournful gleams
That flash and linger of his old-time dreams.

The morning found him where he sank to rest
Within the mystic circle: on his breast
With withered hands, as to the dearest place,
He held and pressed the empty carven case.

That day he sought the dwellings of his folk;
And when he found them, once again there broke

The far-off light upon him, and he cried
From that wrecked cabin threshold for a guide
To lead him, old and weary, to his own.
And surely some kind spirit heard his moan,
And led him to the graves where they were laid.
The evening found him in the tuads' shade,
And like a child at work upon the spot
Where they were sleeping, though he knew it not.

Next day the children found him, and they gazed
In fear at first, for they were sore amazed
To see a man so old they never knew,
Whose garb was savage, and whose white hair grew
And flowed upon his shoulders; but their awe
Was changed to love and pity when they saw
The simple work he wrought at; and they came
And gathered flowers for him, and asked his name,
And laughed at his strange language; and he smiled
To hear them laugh, as though himself a child.

Ere that brief day was o'er, from far and near
The children gathered, wondering; and though
fear
Of scenes a long time shunned at first restrained,
The spell was broken, and soon naught remained
But gladsome features, where of old was dearth
Of happy things and cheery sounds of mirth.
The lizards fled, the snakes and bright-eyed things
Found other homes, where childhood never sings;
And all because poor Jacob, old and wild,
White-haired and fur-clad, was himself a child.
Each day he lived amid these scenes, his ear
Heard far-off voices growing still more clear;
And that dim light that first he saw in gleams
Now left him only in his troubled dreams.

From far away the children loved to come
And play and work with Jacob at his home.
He learned their simple words with childish lip,
And told them often of a white-sailed ship
That sailed across a mighty sea, and found
A beauteous harbor, all encircled round

With flowers and tall green trees; but when they
asked
What did the shipmen then, his mind was tasked
Beyond its strength, and Jacob shook his head,
And with them laughed, for all he knew was said.

The brawny sawyers often ceased their toil,
As Jacob with the children passed, to smile
With rugged pity on their simple play;
Then, gazing after the glad group, would say
How strange it was to see that snowy hair
And time-worn figure with the children fair.

So Jacob Eibsen lived through years of joy, —
A patriarch in age, in heart a boy.
Unto the last he told them of the sea
And white-sailed ship; and ever lovingly,
Unto the end, the garden he had made
He tended daily, 'neath the tuads' shade.

But one bright morning, when the children came
And roused the echoes calling Jacob's name,

The echoes only answered back the sound.
They sought within the huts, but nothing found
Save loneliness and shadow, falling chill
On every sunny searcher: boding ill,
They tried each well-known haunt, and every throat
Sent far abroad the bushman's cooing note.
But all in vain their searching: twilight fell,
And sent them home their sorrowing tale to tell.
That night their elders formed a torch-lit chain
To sweep the gloomy bush; and not in vain, —
For when the moon at midnight hung o'erhead,
The weary searchers found poor Jacob — dead!

He lay within the tuad ring, his face
Laid earthward on his hands; and all the place
Was dim with shadow where the people stood.
And as they gathered there, the circling wood
Seemed filled with awful whisperings, and stirred
By things unseen; and every bushman heard,
From where the corse lay plain within their sight,
A woman's heart-wail rising on the night.

For over all the darkness and the fear
That marked his life from childhood, shining clear,
An arch, like God's bright rainbow, stretched
    above,
And joined the first and last, — his mother's love.

They dug a grave beneath the tuads' shade,
Where all unknown to them the bones were laid
Of Jacob's kindred ; and a prayer was said
In earnest sorrow for the unknown dead,
Round which the children grouped.

                                        Upon the breast
The hands were folded in eternal rest;
But still they held, as dearest to that place
Where life last throbbed, the empty carven case.

THE DOG GUARD.

Nation of sun and sin,
Thy flowers and crimes are red,
And thy heart is sore within
While the glory crowns thy head.
Land of the songless birds,
What was thine ancient crime,
Burning through lapse of time
Like a prophet's cursing words?

Aloes and myrrh and tears
Mix in thy bitter wine:
Drink, while the cup is thine,
Drink, for the draught is sign
Of thy reign in the coming years.

THE DOG GUARD: AN AUSTRALIAN STORY.

THERE are lonesome places upon the earth
That have never re-echoed a sound of mirth,
Where the spirits abide that feast and quaff
On the shuddering soul of a murdered laugh,
And take grim delight in the fearful start,
As their unseen fingers clutch the heart,
And the blood flies out from the griping pain,
To carry the chill through every vein;
And the staring eyes and the whitened faces
Are a joy to these ghosts of the lonesome places.

But of all the spots on this earthly sphere
Where these dismal spirits are strong and near,
There is one more dreary than all the rest,—
'Tis the barren island of Rottenest.
On Australia's western coast, you may—
On a seaman's chart of Fremantle Bay—

Find a tiny speck, some ten miles from shore:
If the chart be good, there is something more,—
For a shoal runs in on the landward side,
With five fathoms marked for the highest tide.
You have nought but my word for all the rest,
But that speck is the island of Rottenest.

'Tis a white sand-heap, about two miles long,
And say half as wide; but the deeds of wrong
Between man and his brother that there took place
Are sufficient to sully a continent's face.
Ah, cruel tales! were they told as a whole,
They would scare your polished humanity's soul;
They would blanch the cheeks in your carpeted
room,
With a terrible thought of the merited doom
For the crimes committed, still unredrest,
On that white sand-heap called Rottenest.

Of late years the island is not so bare
As it was when I saw it first; for there
On the outer headland some buildings stand,

And a flag, red-crossed, says the patch of sand
Is a recognized part of the wide domain
That is blessed with the peace of Victoria's reign.
But behind the lighthouse the land 's the same,
And it bears grim proof of the white man's shame;
For the miniature vales that the island owns
Have a horrible harvest of human bones!

And how did they come there? that 's the word;
And I 'll answer it now with the tale I heard
From the lips of a man who was there, and saw
The bad end of man's greed and of colony law.

Many years ago, when the white man first
Set his foot on the coast, and was hated and cursed
By the native, who had not yet learned to fear
The dark wrath of the stranger, but drove his spear
With a freeman's force and a bushman's yell
At the white invader, it then befell
That so many were killed and cooked and eaten,
There was risk of the whites in the end being
beaten;

So a plan was proposed,—'twas deemed safest and best
To imprison the natives in Rottenest.

And so every time there was white blood spilled,
There were black men captured; and those not killed
In the rage of vengeance were sent away
To this bleak sand isle in Fremantle Bay;
And it soon came round that a thousand men
Were together there, like wild beasts in a pen.
There was not a shrub or grass-blade in the sand,
Nor a piece of timber as large as your hand;
But a government boat went out each day
To fling meat ashore—and then sailed away.

For a year or so was this course pursued,
Till 'twas noticed that fewer came down for food
When the boat appeared; then a guard lay round
The island one night, and the white men found
That the savages swam at the lowest tide
To the shoal that lay on the landward side,—

'Twas a mile from the beach,—and then waded ashore;
So the settlers met in grave council once more.

That a guard was needed was plain to all;
But nobody answered the Governor's call
For a volunteer watch. They were only a few,
And their wild young farms gave plenty to do;
And the council of settlers was breaking up,
With a dread of the sorrow they 'd have to sup
When the savage, unawed, and for vengeance wild,
Lay await in the wood for the mother and child.
And with doleful countenance each to his neighbor
Told a dreary tale of the world of labor
He had, and said, "Let him watch who can,
I can't;" when there stepped to the front a man
With a hard brown face and a burglar's brow,
Who had learned the secret he uttered now
When he served in the chain-gang in New South Wales.
And he said to them: "Friends, as all else fails,

These 'ere natives are safe as if locked and barred,
If you 'll line that shoal with a mastiff guard!"

And the settlers looked at each other awhile,
Till the wonder toned to a well-pleased smile
When the brown ex-burglar said he knew,
And would show the whole of 'em what to do.

Some three weeks after, the guard was set;
And a native who swam to the shoal was met
By two half-starved dogs, when a mile from shore, —
And, somehow, that native was never seen more.
All the settlers were pleased with the capital plan,
And they voted their thanks to the hard-faced man.
For a year, each day did the government boat
Take the meat to the isle and its guard afloat.
In a line, on the face of the shoal, the dogs
Had a dry house each, on some anchored logs;
And the neck-chain from each stretched just half way

To the next dog's house; right across the Bay
Ran a line that was hideous with horrid sounds
From the hungry throats of two hundred hounds.

So one more year passed, and the brutes on the logs
Had grown more like devils than common dogs.
There was such a hell-chorus by day and night
That the settlers ashore were chilled with fright
When they thought—if that legion should break
 away,
And come in with the tide some fatal day!

But they 'scaped that chance; for a man came in
From the Bush, one day, with a 'possum's skin
To the throat filled up with large pearls he 'd found
To the north, on the shore of the Shark's Bay
 Sound.
And the settlement blazed with a wild commotion
At sight of the gems from the wealthy ocean.

Then the settlers all began to pack
Their tools and tents, and to ask the track

That the bushman followed to strike the spot,—
While the dogs and natives were all forgot.
In two days, from that camp on the River Swan,
To the Shark's Bay Sound had the settlers gone ;
And no merciful feeling did one retard
For the helpless men and their terrible guard.

It were vain to try, in my quiet room,
To write down the truth of the awful doom
That befell those savages prisoned there,
When the pangs of hunger and wild despair
Had nigh made them mad as the fiends outside :
'Tis enough that one night, through the low ebb tide,
Swam nine hundred savages, armed with stones
And with weapons made from their dead friends' bones.
Without ripple or sound, when the moon was gone,
Through the inky water they glided on ;
Swimming deep, and scarce daring to draw a breath,
While the guards, if they saw, were as dumb as death.

'Twas a terrible picture! O God! that the night
Were so black as to cover the horrid sight
From the eyes of the Angel that notes man's ways
In the book that will ope on the Day of Days!

There were screams when they met, — shrill screams of pain!
For each animal swam at the length of his chain,
And with parching throat and in furious mood
Lay awaiting, not men, but his coming food.
There were short, sharp cries, and a line of fleck
As the long fangs sank in the swimmer's neck;
There were gurgling growls mixed with human groans,
For the savages drave the sharpened bones
Through their enemies' ribs, and the bodies sank,
Each dog holding fast with a bone through his flank.

Then those of the natives who 'scaped swam back;
But too late! for scores of the savage pack,
Driven mad by the yells and the sounds of fight,
Had broke loose and followed. On that dread night

4

Let the curtain fall: when the red sun rose
From the placid ocean, the joys and woes
Of a thousand men he had last eve seen
Were as things or thoughts that had never been.

When the settlers returned, — in a month or two, —
They bethought of the dogs and the prisoned crew.
And a boat went out on a tardy quest
Of whatever was living on Rottenest.
They searched all the isle, and sailed back agen
With some specimen bones of the dogs and men.

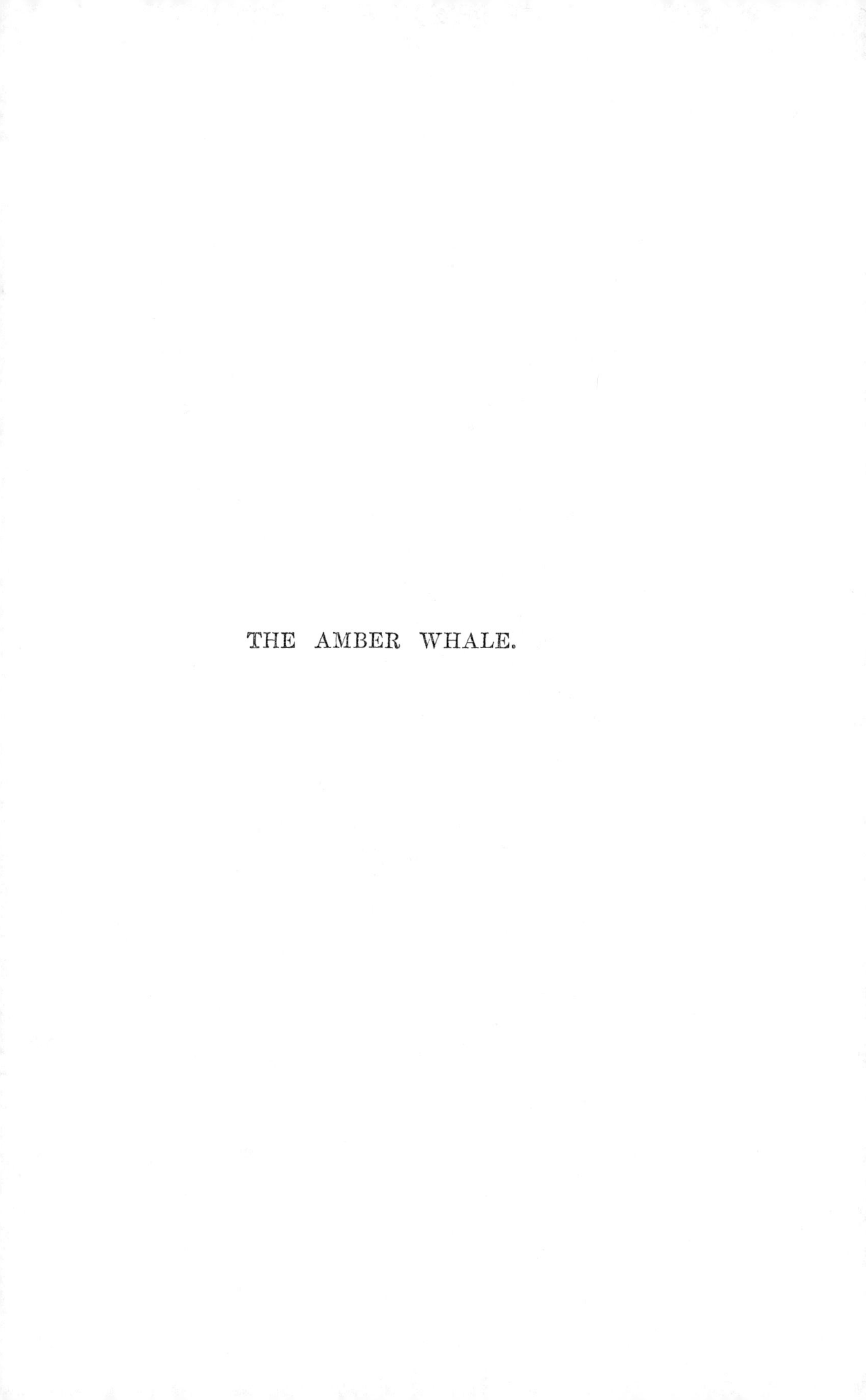

THE AMBER WHALE.

Though it lash the shallows that line the beach,
Afar from the great sea deeps,
There is never a storm whose might can reach
Where the vast leviathan sleeps.
Like a mighty thought in a giant mind,
In the clear, cold depths he swims;
Whilst above him the pettiest form of his kind
With a dash o'er the surface skims.

There is peace in power: the men who speak
With the loudest tongues do least;
And the surest sign of a mind that is weak
Is its want of the power to rest.
It is only the lighter water that flies
From the sea on a windy day;
And the deep blue ocean never replies
To the sibilant voice of the spray.

THE AMBER WHALE: A HARPOONEER'S STORY.

[Whalemen have a strange belief as to the formation of amber. They say that it is a petrifaction of some internal part of a whale; and they tell weird stories of enormous whales seen in the warm latitudes, that were almost entirely transformed into the precious substance.]

WE were down in the Indian Ocean, after sperm, and three years out;
The last six months in the tropics, and looking in vain for a spout, —
Five men up on the royal yards, weary of straining their sight;
And every day like its brother, — just morning and noon and night —
Nothing to break the sameness: water and wind and sun
Motionless, gentle, and blazing, — never a change in one.

Every day like its brother: when the noonday eight-bells came,
'Twas like yesterday; and we seemed to know that to-morrow would be the same.
The foremast hands had a lazy time: there was never a thing to do;
The ship was painted, tarred down, and scraped; and the mates had nothing new.
We 'd worked at sinnet and ratline till there wasn't a yarn to use,
And all we could do was watch and pray for a sperm whale's spout — or news.
It was whaler's luck of the vilest sort; and, though many a volunteer
Spent his watch below on the look-out, never a whale came near, —
At least of the kind we wanted: there were lots of whales of a sort, —
Killers and finbacks, and such like, as if they enjoyed the sport
Of seeing a whale-ship idle; but we never lowered a boat

For less than a blackfish, — there's no oil in a
killer's or finback's coat.
There was rich reward for the look-out men, —
tobacco for even a sail,
And a barrel of oil for the lucky dog who 'd be
first to "raise" a whale.
The crew was a mixture from every land, and many
a tongue they spoke;
And when they sat in the fo'castle, enjoying an
evening smoke,
There were tales told, youngster, would make you
stare, — stories of countless shoals
Of devil-fish in the Pacific and right-whales away
at the Poles.
There was one of these fo'castle yarns that we
always loved to hear, —
Kanaka and Maori and Yankee; all lent an eager
ear
To that strange old tale that was always new, —
the wonderful treasure-tale
Of an old Down-Eastern harpooneer who had
struck an Amber Whale!

Ay, that was a tale worth hearing, lad: if 'twas true we couldn't say,
Or if 'twas a yarn old Mat had spun to while the time away.

"It's just fifteen years ago," said Mat, "since I shipped as harpooneer
On board a bark in New Bedford, and came cruising somewhere near
To this whaling-ground we're cruising now; but whales were plenty then,
And not like now, when we scarce get oil to pay for the ship and men.
There were none of these oil wells running then, — at least, what shore folk term
An oil well in Pennsylvania, — but sulphur-bottom and sperm
Were plenty as frogs in a mud-hole, and all of 'em big whales, too;
One hundred barrels for sperm-whales; and for sulphur-bottom, two.
You couldn't pick out a small one: the littlest calf or cow

Had a sight more oil than the big bull whales we
think so much of now.
We were more to the east, off Java Straits, a little
below the mouth, —
A hundred and five to the east'ard and nine degrees to the south;
And that was as good a whaling-ground for middling-sized, handy whales
As any in all the ocean; and 'twas always white
with sails
From Scotland and Hull and New England, — for
the whales were thick as frogs,
And 'twas little trouble to kill 'em then, for they
lay as quiet as logs.
And every night we 'd go visiting the other whaleships 'round,
Or p'r'aps we 'd strike on a Dutchman, calmed off
the Straits, and bound
To Singapore or Batavia, with plenty of schnapps
to sell
For a few whale's teeth or a gallon of oil, and the
latest news to tell.

And in every ship of that whaling fleet was one
wonderful story told, —
How an Amber Whale had been seen that year
that was worth a mint of gold.
And one man — mate of a Scotchman — said he 'd
seen, away to the west,
A big school of sperm, and one whale's spout was
twice as high as the rest;
And we knew that that was the Amber Whale, for
we 'd often heard before
That his spout was twice as thick as the rest, and
a hundred feet high or more.
And often, when the look-out cried, 'He blows!'
the very hail
Thrilled every heart with the greed of gold, — for
we thought of the Amber Whale.

"But never a sight of his spout we saw till the sea-
son there went round,
And the ships ran down to the south'ard to an-
other whaling-ground.

We stayed to the last off Java, and then we ran
to the west,
To get our recruits at Mauritius, and give the crew
a rest.
Five days we ran in the trade winds, and the boys
were beginning to talk
Of their time ashore, and whether they 'd have a
donkey-ride or a walk,
And whether they 'd spend their money in wine,
bananas, or pearls,
Or drive to the sugar plantations to dance with the
Creole girls.
But they soon got something to talk about. Five
days we ran west-sou'-west,
But the sixth day's log-book entry was a change
from all the rest;
For that was the day the mast-head men made
every face turn pale,
With the cry that we all had dreamt about, — 'HE
BLOWS! THE AMBER WHALE!'

"And every man was motionless, and every speaker's lip
Just stopped as it was, with the word half-said: there wasn't a sound in the ship
Till the Captain hailed the masthead, 'Whereaway is the whale you see?'
And the cry came down again, 'He blows! about four points on our lee,
And three miles off, sir, — there he blows! he 's going to leeward fast!'
And then we sprang to the rigging, and saw the great whale at last!

"Ah! shipmates, that was a sight to see: the water was smooth as a lake,
And there was the monster rolling, with a school of whales in his wake.
They looked like pilot-fish round a shark, as if they were keeping guard;
And, shipmates, the spout of that Amber Whale was high as a sky-sail yard.
There was never a ship's crew worked so quick as our whalemen worked that day, —

When the captain shouted, 'Swing the boats, and
be ready to lower away!'
Then, 'A pull on the weather-braces, men! let her
head fall off three points!'
And off she swung, with a quarter-breeze straining
the old ship's joints.
The men came down from the mastheads; and the
boats' crews stood on the rail,
Stowing the lines and irons, and fixing paddles and
sail.
And when all was ready we leant on the boats and
looked at the Amber's spout,
That went up like a monster fountain, with a sort
of a rumbling shout,
Like a thousand railroad engines puffing away their
smoke.
He was just like a frigate's hull capsized, and the
swaying water broke
Against the sides of the great stiff whale: he was
steering south-by-west, —
For the Cape, no doubt, for a whale can shape a
course as well as the best.

We soon got close as was right to go; for the school
might hear a hail,
Or see the bark, and that was the last of our Bank-
of-England Whale.
'Let her luff,' said the Old Man, gently. 'Now,
lower away, my boys,
And pull for a mile, then paddle, — and mind that
you make no noise.'

"A minute more, and the boats were down; and
out from the hull of the bark
They shot with a nervous sweep of the oars, like
dolphins away from a shark.
Each officer stood in the stern, and watched, as he
held the steering oar,
And the crews bent down to their pulling as they
never pulled before.

"Our Mate was as thorough a whaleman as I ever
met afloat;
And I was his harpooneer that day, and sat in the
bow of the boat.

His eyes were set on the whales ahead, and he spoke
in a low, deep tone,
And told the men to be steady and cool, and the
whale was all our own.
And steady and cool they proved to be: you could
read it in every face,
And in every straining muscle, that they meant to
win that race.
'Bend to it, boys, for a few strokes more, — bend to
it steady and long!
Now, in with your oars, and paddles out, — all
together, and strong!'
Then we turned and sat on the gunwale, with our
faces to the bow;
And the whales were right ahead, — no more than
four ships' lengths off now.
There were five of 'em, hundred-barrellers, like
guards round the Amber Whale.
And to strike him we 'd have to risk being stove by
crossing a sweeping tail;
But the prize and the risk were equal. 'Mat,' now
whispers the Mate,

'Are your irons ready?' 'Ay, ay, sir.' 'Stand up, then, steady, and wait
Till I give the word, then let 'em fly, and hit him below the fin
As he rolls to wind'ard. Start her, boys! now 's the time to slide her in!
Hurrah! that fluke just missed us. Mind, as soon as the iron 's fast,
Be ready to back your paddles, — now in for it, boys, at last.
Heave! Again!'

"And two irons flew: the first one sank in the joint,
'Tween the head and hump, — in the muscle; but the second had its point
Turned off by striking the amber case, coming out again like a bow,
And the monster carcass quivered, and rolled with pain from the first deep blow.
Then he lashed the sea with his terrible flukes, and showed us many a sign

That his rage was roused. 'Lay off,' roared the
Mate, 'and all keep clear of the line!'
And that was a timely warning, for the whale made
an awful breach
Right out of the sea; and 'twas well for us that the
boat was beyond the reach
Of his sweeping flukes, as he milled around, and
made for the Captain's boat,
That was right astern. And, shipmates, then my
heart swelled up in my throat
At the sight I saw: the Amber Whale was lash-
ing the sea with rage,
And two of his hundred-barrel guards were ready
now to engage
In a bloody fight, and with open jaws they came
to their master's aid.
Then we knew the Captain's boat was doomed; but
the crew were no whit afraid, —
They were brave New England whalemen, — and
we saw the harpooneer
Stand up to send in his irons, as soon as the whales
came near.

Then we heard the Captain's order, 'Heave!' and
saw the harpoon fly,
As the whales closed in with their open jaws: a
shock, and a stifled cry
Was all that we heard; then we looked to see if
the crew were still afloat,—
But nothing was there save a dull red patch, and
the boards of the shattered boat!

"But that was no time for mourning words: the
other two boats came in,
And one got fast on the quarter, and one aft the
starboard fin
Of the Amber Whale. For a minute he paused, as
if he were in doubt
As to whether 'twas best to run or fight. 'Lay
on!' the Mate roared out,
'And I'll give him a lance!' The boat shot in;
and the Mate, when he saw his chance
Of sending it home to the vitals, four times he
buried his lance.
A minute more, and a cheer went up, when we saw
that his aim was good;

For the lance had struck in a life-spot, and the whale
was spouting blood!
But now came the time of danger, for the school of
whales around
Had aired their flukes, and the cry was raised,
'Look out! they're going to sound!'
And down they went with a sudden plunge, the
Amber Whale the last,
While the lines ran smoking out of the tubs, he
went to the deep so fast.
Before you could count your fingers, a hundred
fathoms were out;
And then he stopped, for a wounded whale must
come to the top and spout.
We hauled slack line as we felt him rise; and
when he came up alone,
And spouted thick blood, we cheered again, for we
knew he was all our own.
He was frightened now, and his fight was gone,—
right round and round he spun,
As if he was trying to sight the boats, or find the
best side to run.

But that was the minute for us to work: the boats
hauled in their slack,
And bent on the drag-tubs over the stern to tire
and hold him back.
The bark was five miles to wind'ard, and the mate
gave a troubled glance
At the sinking sun, and muttered, 'Boys, we must
give him another lance,
Or he 'll run till night; and, if he should head to
wind'ard in the dark,
We 'll be forced to cut loose and leave him, or else
lose run of the bark.'
So we hauled in close, two boats at once, but only
frightened the whale;
And, like a hound that was badly whipped, he
turned and showed his tail,
With his head right dead to wind'ard; then as
straight and as swift he sped
As a hungry shark for a swimming prey; and,
bending over his head,
Like a mighty plume, went his bloody spout. Ah!
shipmates, that was a sight

Worth a life at sea to witness. In his wake the sea
was white
As you 've seen it after a steamer's screw, churning
up like foaming yeast;
And the boats went hissing along at the rate of
twenty knots at least,
With the water flush with the gunwale, and the
oars were all apeak,
While the crews sat silent and quiet, watching the
long, white streak
That was traced by the line of our passage. We
hailed the bark as we passed,
And told them to keep a sharp look-out from the
head of every mast;
'And if we 're not back by sundown,' cried the
Mate, 'you keep a light
At the royal cross-trees. If he dies, we may stick
to the whale all night.'

"And past we swept with our oars apeak, and
waved our hands to the hail
Of the wondering men on the taffrail, who were
watching our Amber Whale

As he surged ahead, just as if he thought he could
tire his enemies out;
I was almost sorrowful, shipmates, to see after each
red spout
That the great whale's strength was failing: the
sweep of his flukes grew slow,
Till at sundown he made about four knots, and his
spout was weak and low.
Then said the Mate to his boat's crew: 'Boys, the
vessel is out of sight
To the leeward: now, shall we cut the line, or stick
to the whale all night?'
'We'll stick to the whale!' cried every man. 'Let
the other boats go back
To the vessel and beat to wind'ard, as well as they
can, in our track.'
It was done as they said: the lines were cut, and
the crews cried out, 'Good speed!'
As we swept along in the darkness, in the wake
of our monster steed,
That went plunging on, with the dogged hope that
he'd tire his enemies still,—

But even the strength of an Amber Whale must
break before human will.
By little and little his power had failed as he
spouted his blood away,
Till at midnight the rising moon shone down on
the great fish as he lay
Just moving his flukes; but at length he stopped,
and raising his square, black head
As high as the topmast cross-trees, swung round
and fell over — dead!

"And then rose a shout of triumph, — a shout that
was more like a curse
Than an honest cheer; but, shipmates, the thought
in our hearts was worse,
And 'twas punished with bitter suffering. We
claimed the whale as our own,
And said that the crew should have no share of the
wealth that was ours alone.
We said to each other: We want their help till we
get the whale aboard,
So we'll let 'em think that they'll have a share till
we get the Amber stored,

And then we 'll pay them their wages, and send
them ashore — *or afloat,*
If they show their temper. Ah! shipmates, no
wonder 'twas that boat
And its selfish crew were cursed that night. Next
day we saw no sail,
But the wind and sea were rising. Still, we held
to the drifting whale, —
And a dead whale drifts to windward, — going
farther away from the ship,
Without water, or bread, or courage to pray with
heart or lip
That had planned and spoken the treachery. The
wind blew into a gale,
And it screamed like mocking laughter round our
boat and the Amber Whale.

" That night fell dark on the starving crew, and a
hurricane blew next day;
Then we cut the line, and we cursed the prize as it
drifted fast away,
As if some power under the waves were towing it
out of sight;

And there we were, without help or hope, dreading
the coming night.
Three days that hurricane lasted. When it passed,
two men were dead;
And the strongest one of the living had not strength
to raise his head,
When his dreaming swoon was broken by the sound
of a cheery hail,
And he saw a shadow fall on the boat, — it fell
from the old bark's sail!
And when he heard their kindly words, you 'd think
he should have smiled
With joy at his deliverance; but he cried like a
little child,
And hid his face in his poor weak hands, — for he
thought of the selfish plan, —
And he prayed to God to forgive them all. And,
shipmates, I am the man! —
The only one of the sinful crew that ever beheld
his home;
For before the cruise was over, all the rest were
under the foam.

It 's just fifteen years gone, shipmates," said old
Mat, ending his tale ;
"And I often pray that I 'll never see another
Amber Whale."

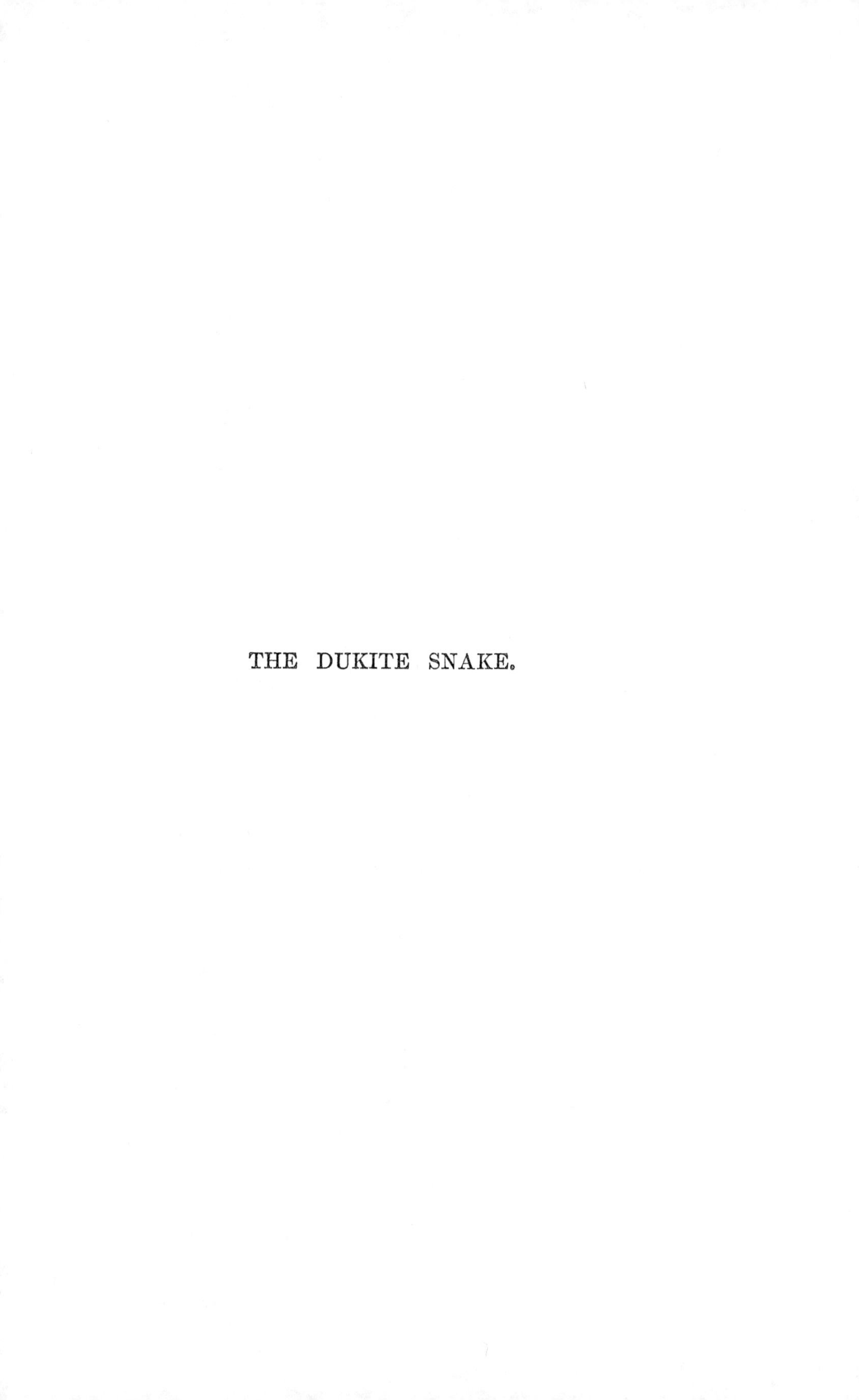

THE DUKITE SNAKE.

Love is a plant with double root,
And of strange elastic power:
Men's minds are divided in naming the fruit,
But a kiss is only the flower.

THE DUKITE SNAKE:

A WEST AUSTRALIAN BUSHMAN'S STORY.

WELL, mate, you 've asked me about a fellow
You met to-day, in a black-and-yellow
Chain-gang suit, with a pedler's pack,
Or with some such burden, strapped to his back.
Did you meet him square? No, passed you by?
Well, if you had, and had looked in his eye,
You 'd have felt for your irons then and there;
For the light in his eye is a madman's glare.
Ay, mad, poor fellow! I know him well,
And if you 're not sleepy just yet, I 'll tell
His story,—a strange one as ever you heard
Or read; but I 'll vouch for it, every word.

You just wait a minute, mate: I must see
How that damper 's doing, and make some tea.

You smoke? That 's good; for there 's plenty of
weed
In that wallaby skin. Does your horse feed
In the hobbles? Well, he 's got good feed here,
And my own old bushmare won't interfere.
Done with that meat? Throw it there to the
dogs,
And fling on a couple of banksia logs.

And now for the story. That man who goes
Through the bush with the pack and the convict's
clothes
Has been mad for years; but he does no harm,
And our lonely settlers feel no alarm
When they see or meet him. Poor Dave Sloane
Was a settler once, and a friend of my own.
Some eight years back, in the spring of the year,
Dave came from Scotland, and settled here.
A splendid young fellow he was just then,
And one of the bravest and truest men
That I ever met: he was kind as a woman
To all who needed a friend, and no man —

Not even a convict — met with his scorn,
For David Sloane was a gentleman born.
Ay, friend, a gentleman, though it sounds queer :
There 's plenty of blue blood flowing out here,
And some younger sons of your "upper ten"
Can be met with here, first-rate bushmen.
Why, friend, *I*—
Bah! curse that dog! you see
This talking so much has affected me.

Well, Sloane came here with an axe and a gun;
He bought four miles of a sandal-wood run.
This bush at that time was a lonesome place,
So lonesome the sight of a white man's face
Was a blessing, unless it came at night,
And peered in your hut, with the cunning fright
Of a runaway convict; and even they
Were welcome, for talk's sake, while they could stay.
Dave lived with me here for a while, and learned
The tricks of the bush, — how the snare was laid
In the wallaby track, how traps were made,

How 'possums and kangaroo rats were killed;
And when that was learned, I helped him to build
From mahogany slabs a good bush hut,
And showed him how sandal-wood logs were cut.
I lived up there with him days and days,
For I loved the lad for his honest ways.
I had only one fault to find: at first
Dave worked too hard; for a lad who was nursed,
As he was, in idleness, it was strange
How he cleared that sandal-wood off his range.
From the morning light till the light expired
He was always working, he never tired;
Till at length I began to think his will
Was too much settled on wealth, and still
When I looked at the lad's brown face, and eye
Clear open, my heart gave such thought the lie.
But one day — for he read my mind — he laid
His hand on my shoulder: "Don't be afraid,"
Said he, "that I 'm seeking alone for pelf.
I work hard, friend; but 'tis not for myself."

And he told me then, in his quiet tone,
Of a girl in Scotland, who was his own, —

His wife, — 'twas for her: 'twas all he could say,
And his clear eye brimmed as he turned away.
After that he told me the simple tale:
They had married for love, and she was to sail
For Australia when he wrote home and told
The oft-watched-for story of finding gold.

In a year he wrote, and his news was good:
He had bought some cattle and sold his wood.
He said, "Darling, I 've only a hut, — but come."
Friend, a husband's heart is a true wife's home;
And he knew she 'd come. Then he turned his hand
To make neat the house, and prepare the land
For his crops and vines; and he made that place
Put on such a smiling and homelike face,
That when she came, and he showed her round
His sandal-wood and his crops in the ground,
And spoke of the future, they cried for joy,
The husband's arm clasping his wife and boy.

Well, friend, if a little of heaven's best bliss
Ever comes from the upper world to this,

It came into that manly bushman's life,
And circled him round with the arms of his wife.
God bless that bright memory! Even to me,
A rough, lonely man, did she seem to be,
While living, an angel of God's pure love,
And now I could pray to her face above.
And David he loved her as only a man
With a heart as large as was his heart can.
I wondered how they could have lived apart,
For he was her idol, and she his heart.

Friend, there isn't much more of the tale to tell:
I was talking of angels awhile since. Well,
Now I'll change to a devil, — ay, to a devil!
You need n't start: if a spirit of evil
Ever came to this world its hate to slake
On mankind, it came as a Dukite Snake.

Like? Like the pictures you've seen of Sin,
A long red snake, — as if what was within
Was fire that gleamed through his glistening
skin.

And his eyes! — if you could go down to hell
And come back to your fellows here and tell
What the fire was like, you could find no thing,
Here below on the earth, or up in the sky,
To compare it to but a Dukite's eye!

Now, mark you, these Dukites don't go alone:
There 's another near when you see but one;
And beware you of killing that one you see
Without finding the other; for you may be
More than twenty miles from the spot that night,
When camped, but you 're tracked by the lone
Dukite,
That will follow your trail like Death or Fate,
And kill you as sure as you killed its mate!

Well, poor Dave Sloane had his young wife here
Three months, — 'twas just this time of the year.
He had teamed some sandal-wood to the Vasse,
And was homeward bound, when he saw in the
grass
A long red snake: he had never been told

Of the Dukite's ways, — he jumped to the road,
And smashed its flat head with the bullock-goad!

He was proud of the red skin, so he tied
Its tail to the cart, and the snake's blood dyed
The bush on the path he followed that night.

He was early home, and the dead Dukite
Was flung at the door to be skinned next day.
At sunrise next morning he started away
To hunt up his cattle. A three hours' ride
Brought him back: he gazed on his home with pride
And joy in his heart; he jumped from his horse
And entered — to look on his young wife's corse,
And his dead child clutching its mother's clothes
As in fright; and there, as he gazed, arose
From her breast, where 'twas resting, the gleaming head
Of the terrible Dukite, as if it said,
"*I've had vengeance, my foe: you took all I had.*"

And so had the snake — David Sloane was mad!

I rode to his hut just by chance that night,
And there on the threshold the clear moonlight
Showed the two snakes dead. I pushed in the
door
With an awful feeling of coming woe:
The dead were stretched on the moonlit floor,
The man held the hand of his wife, — his pride,
His poor life's treasure, — and crouched by her
side.
O God! I sank with the weight of the blow.
I touched and called him: he heeded me not,
So I dug her grave in a quiet spot,
And lifted them both, — her boy on her breast, —
And laid them down in the shade to rest.
Then I tried to take my poor friend away,
But he cried so wofully, "Let me stay
Till she comes again!" that I had no heart
To try to persuade him then to part
From all that was left to him here, — her grave;
So I stayed by his side that night, and, save
One heart-cutting cry, he uttered no sound, —
O God! that wail — like the wail of a hound!

'Tis six long years since I heard that cry,
But 'twill ring in my ears till the day I die.
Since that fearful night no one has heard
Poor David Sloane utter sound or word.
You have seen to-day how he always goes:
He 's been given that suit of convict's clothes
By some prison officer. On his back
You noticed a load like a pedler's pack?
Well, that 's what he lives for: when reason went,
Still memory lived, for his days are spent
In searching for Dukites; and year by year
That bundle of skins is growing. 'Tis clear
That the Lord out of evil some good still takes;
For he 's clearing this bush of the Dukite snakes.

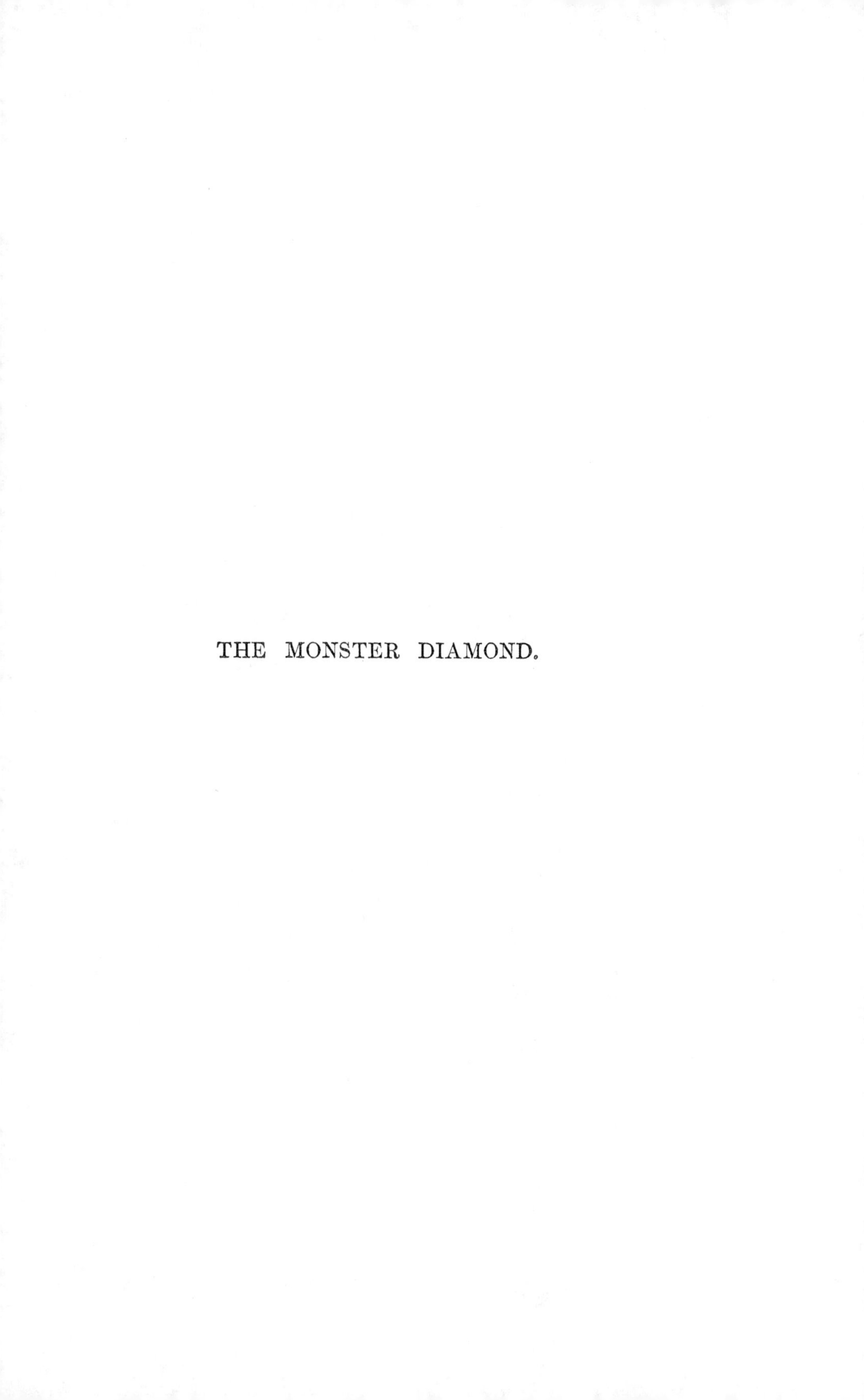

THE MONSTER DIAMOND.

Each virtuous act is a kernel sown
That will grow to a goodly tree,
Shedding its fruit when time has flown
Down the gulf of eternity.

THE MONSTER DIAMOND:

A TALE OF THE PENAL COLONY OF WEST AUSTRALIA.

"I 'LL have it, I tell you! Curse you!—there!"
The long knife glittered, was sheathed, and
was bare.
The sawyer staggered and tripped and fell,
And falling he uttered a frightened yell:
His face to the sky, he shuddered and gasped,
And tried to put from him the man he had grasped
A moment before in the terrible strife.
"I'll have it, I tell you, or have your life!
Where is it?" The sawyer grew weak, but still
His brown face gleamed with a desperate will.
"Where is it?" he heard, and the red knife's drip
In his slayer's hand fell down on his lip.
"Will you give it?" "Never!" A curse, the knife
Was raised and buried.

Thus closed the life
Of Samuel Jones, known as "Number Ten"
On his Ticket-of-Leave; and of all the men
In the Western Colony, bond or free,
None had manlier heart or hand than he.

In digging a sawpit, while all alone,—
For his mate was sleeping,—Sam struck a stone
With the edge of the spade, and it gleamed like
fire,
And looked at Sam from its bed in the mire,
Till he dropped the spade and stooped and raised
The wonderful stone that glittered and blazed
As if it were mad at the spade's rude blow;
But its blaze set the sawyer's heart aglow
As he looked and trembled, then turned him round,
And crept from the pit, and lay on the ground,
Looking over the mould-heap at the camp
Where his mate still slept. Then down to the
swamp
He ran with the stone, and washed it bright,
And felt like a drunken man at the sight

Of a diamond pure as spring-water and sun,
And larger than ever man's eyes looked on!

Then down sat Sam with the stone on his knees,
And fancies came to him, like swarms of bees
To a sugar-creamed hive; and he dreamed awake
Of the carriage and four in which he 'd take
His pals from the Dials to Drury Lane,
The silks and the satins for Susan Jane,
The countless bottles of brandy and beer
He 'd call for and pay for, and every year
The dinner he 'd give to the Brummagem lads,—
He 'd be king among cracksmen and chief among pads,
And he 'd sport a —

Over him stooped his mate,
A pick in his hand, and his face all hate.
Sam saw the shadow, and guessed the pick,
And closed his dream with a spring so quick
The purpose was baffled of Aaron Mace,
And the sawyer mates stood face to face.

Sam folded his arms across his chest,
Having thrust the stone in his loose shirt-breast,
While he tried to think where he dropped the spade.
But Aaron Mace wore a long, keen blade
In his belt, — he drew it, — sprang on his man:
What happened, you read when the tale began.

Then he looked — the murderer, Aaron Mace —
At the gray-blue lines in the dead man's face;
And he turned away, for he feared its frown
More in death than life. Then he knelt him down, —
Not to pray, — but he shrank from the staring eyes,
And felt in the breast for the fatal prize.
And this was the man, and this was the way
That he took the stone on its natal day;
And for this he was cursed for evermore
By the West Australian Koh-i-nor.

In the half-dug pit the corpse was thrown,
And the murderer stood in the camp alone.
Alone? No, no! never more was he
To part from the terrible company

Of that gray-blue face and the bleeding breast
And the staring eyes in their awful rest.
The evening closed on the homicide,
And the blood of the buried sawyer cried
Through the night to God, and the shadows dark,
That crossed the camp had the stiff and stark
And horrible look of a murdered man!
Then he piled the fire, and crept within
The ring of its light, that closed him in
Like tender mercy, and drove away
For a time the spectres that stood at bay,
And waited to clutch him as demons wait,
Shut out from the sinner by Faith's bright gate.
But the fire burnt low, and the slayer slept,
And the key of his sleep was always kept
By the leaden hand of him he had slain,
That oped the door but to drench the brain
With agony cruel. The night wind crept
Like a snake on the shuddering form that slept
And dreamt, and woke and shrieked; for there,
With its gray-blue lines and its ghastly stare,

Cutting into the vitals of Aaron Mace,
In the flickering light was the sawyer's face!

Evermore 'twas with him, that dismal sight, —
The white face set in the frame of night.
He wandered away from the spot, but found
No inch of the West Australian ground
Where he could hide from the bleeding breast,
Or sink his head in a dreamless rest.

And always with him he bore the prize
In a pouch of leather: the staring eyes
Might burn his soul, but the diamond's gleam
Was solace and joy for the haunted dream.

So the years rolled on, while the murderer's mind
Was bent on a futile quest, — to find
A way of escape from the blood-stained soil
And the terrible wear of the penal toil.

But this was a part of the diamond's curse, —
The toil that was heavy before grew worse,

Till the panting wretch in his fierce unrest
Would clutch the pouch as it lay on his breast,
And waking cower, with sob and moan,
Or shriek wild curses against the stone
That was only a stone; for he could not sell,
And he dare not break, and he feared to tell
Of his wealth: so he bore it through hopes and fears —
His God and his devil — for years and years.

And thus did he draw near the end of his race,
With a form bent double and horror-lined face,
And a piteous look, as if asking for grace
Or for kindness from some one; but no kind word
Was flung to his misery: shunned, abhorred,
E'en by wretches themselves, till his life was a curse,
And he thought that e'en death could bring nothing worse
Than the phantoms that stirred at the diamond's weight, —
His own life's ghost and the ghost of his mate.

So he turned one day from the haunts of men,
And their friendless faces: an old man then,
In a convict's garb, with white flowing hair,
And a brow deep seared with the word, "Despair."
He gazed not back as his way he took
To the untrod forest; and oh! the look,
The piteous look in his sunken eyes,
Told that life was the bitterest sacrifice.

But little was heard of his later days:
'Twas deemed in the West that in change of ways
He tried with his tears to wash out the sin.
'Twas told by some natives who once came in
From the Kojunup Hills, that lonely there
They had seen a figure with long white hair;
They encamped close by where his hut was made,
And were scared at night when they saw he prayed
To the white man's God; and on one wild night
They had heard his voice till the morning light.

Years passed, and a sandalwood-cutter stood
At a ruined hut in a Kojunup wood:

The rank weeds covered the desolate floor,
And an ant-hill stood on the fallen door;
The cupboard within to the snakes was loot,
And the hearth was the home of the bandicoot.
But neither at hut nor snake nor rat
Was the woodcutter staring intent, but at
A human skeleton clad in gray,
The hands clasped over the breast, as they
Had fallen in peace when he ceased to pray.

As the bushman looked on the form, he saw
In the breast a paper: he stooped to draw
What might tell him the story, but at his touch
From under the hands rolled a leathern pouch,
And he raised it too, — on the paper's face
He read "Ticket-of-Leave of Aaron Mace."
Then he opened the pouch, and in dazed surprise
At its contents strange he unblessed his eyes:
'*Twas a lump of quartz*, — a pound weight in full, —
And it fell from his hand on the skeleton's skull!

HAUNTED BY TIGERS.

NATHAN BEANS and William Lambert were
two wild New England boys,
Known from infancy to revel only in forbidden
joys.
Many a mother of Nantucket bristled when she
heard them come,
With a horrid skulking whistle, tempting her good
lad from home.
But for all maternal bristling little did they seem to
care,
And they loved each other dearly, did this good-for-
nothing pair.

So they lived till eighteen summers found them in
the same repute, —
They had well-developed muscles, and loose char-
acters to boot.

Then they did what wild Nantucket boys have
never failed to do, —
Went and filled two oily bunks among a whaler's
oily crew.
And the mothers, — ah! they raised their hands
and blessed the lucky day,
While Nantucket waved its handkerchief to see
them sail away.

On a four years' cruise they started in the brave old
"Patience Parr,"
And were soon initiated in the mysteries of tar.
There they found the truth that whalers' tales are
unsubstantial wiles, —
They were sick and sore and sorry ere they passed
the Western Isles;
And their captain, old-man Sculpin, gave their
fancies little scope,
For he argued with a marlinspike and reasoned
with a rope.

But they stuck together bravely, they were Ish-
maels with the crew:

Nathan's voice was never raised but Bill's support
was uttered too;
And whenever Beans was floored by Sculpin's cruel
marlinspike,
Down beside him went poor Lambert, for his hand
was clenched to strike.
So they passed two years in cruising, till one breath-
less burning day
The old "Patience Parr" in Sunda Straits * with
flapping canvas lay.
On her starboard side Sumatra's woods were dark
beneath the glare,
And on her port stretched Java, slumbering in the
yellow air, —
Slumbering as the jaguar slumbers, as the tropic
ocean sleeps,
Smooth and smiling on its surface with a devil in
its deeps.
So swooned Java's moveless forest, but the jungle
round its root

* The Straits of Sunda, seven miles wide at the southern extremity, lie between Sumatra and Java.

Knew the rustling anaconda and the tiger's padded
foot.
There in Nature's rankest garden, Nature's worst
alone is rife,
And a glorious land is wild-beast ruled for want of
human life.
Scarce a harmless thing moved on it, not a living
soul was near
From the frowning rocks of Java Head right north-
ward to Anjier.
Crestless swells, like wind-raised canvas, made the
whaler rise and dip,
Else she lay upon the water like a paralytic
ship;
And beneath a topsail awning lay the lazy, languid
crew,
Drinking in the precious coolness of the shadow, —
all save two:
Two poor Ishmaels, — they were absent, Heaven
help them ! — roughly tied
'Neath the blistering cruel sun-glare in the fore-
chains, side by side.

Side by side as it was always, each one with a
word of cheer
For the other, and for his sake bravely choking
back the tear.
Side by side, their pain or pastime never yet seemed
good for one;
But whenever pain came, each in secret wished the
other gone.

You who stop at home and saunter o'er your flower-
scattered path,
With life's corners velvet-cushioned, have you seen
a tyrant's wrath?—
Wrath, the rude and reckless demon, not the
drawing-room display
Of an anger led by social lightning-rods upon its
way.
Ah! my friends, wrath's raw materials on the land
may sometimes be,
But the manufactured article is only found at sea.

And the wrath of old-man Sculpin was of texture
Number One:

Never absent, — when the man smiled it was hidden, but not gone.
Old church-members of Nantucket knew him for a shining lamp,
But his chronic Christian spirit was of pharisaic stamp.
When ashore, he prayed aloud of how he 'd sinned and been forgiven, —
How his evil ways had brought him 'thin an ace of losing heaven;
Thank the Lord! his eyes were opened, and so on; but when the ship
Was just ready for a voyage, you could see old Sculpin's lip
Have a sort of nervous tremble, like a carter's long-leashed whip
Ere it cracks; and so the skipper's lip was trembling for an oath
At the watch on deck for idleness, the watch below for sloth,
For the leash of his anathemas was long enough for both.

Well, 'twas burning noon off Java: Beans and
Lambert in the chains
Sank their heads, and all was silent but the voices
of their pains.
Night came ere their bonds were loosened; then
the boys sank down and slept,
And the dew in place of loved ones on their
wounded bodies wept.

All was still within the whaler, — on the sea no
fanning breeze,
And the moon alone was moving over Java's gloomy
trees.
Midnight came, — one sleeper's waking glance went
out the moon to meet:
Nathan rose, and turned from Lambert, who still
slumbered at his feet.
Out toward Java went his vision, as if something
in the air
Came with promises of kindness and of peace to
be found there.

Then towards the davits moved he, where the
    lightest whale-boat hung;
And he worked with silent caution till upon the
    sea she swung,
When he paused, and looked at Lambert, and the
    spirit in him cried
Not to leave him, but to venture, as since child-
    hood, side by side;
And the spirit's cry was answered, for he touched
    the sleeper's lip,
Who awoke and heard of Nathan's plan to leave
    th' accursed ship.

When 'twas told, they rose in silence, and looked
    outward to the land,
But they only saw Nantucket, with its homely,
    boat-lined strand;
But they saw it — oh! so plainly — through the
    glass of coming doom.
Then they crept into the whale-boat, and pulled
    toward the forest's gloom, —
All their suffering clear that moment, like the
    moonlight on their wake,

Now contracting, now expanding, like a phospho-
rescent snake.
Hours speed on: the dark horizon yet shows scarce
a streak of gray
When old Sculpin comes on deck to walk his rest-
lessness away.
All the scene is still and solemn, and mayhap the
man's cold heart
Feels its teaching, for the wild-beast cries from
shoreward make him start
As if they had warning in them, and he o'er its
meaning pored,
Till at length one shriek from Java splits the dark-
ness like a sword;
And he almost screams in answer, such the nearness
of the cry,
As he clutches at the rigging with a horror in his
eye,
And with faltering accents mutters, as against the
mast he leans,
"*Darn the tigers! that one shouted with the voice of
Nathan Beans!*"

When the boys were missed soon after, Sculpin never breathed a word
Of his terror in the morning at the fearful sound he 'd heard;
But he entered in the log-book, and 'twas witnessed by the mates,
Just their names, and following after, "Ran away in Sunda Straits."

Two years after, Captain Sculpin saw again the Yankee shore,
With the comfortable feeling that he 'd go to sea no more.
And 'twas strange the way he altered when he saw Nantucket light:
Holy lines spread o'er his face, and chased the old ones out of sight.
And for many a year thereafter did his zeal spread far and wide,
And with all his pious doings was the township edified;

For he led the sacred singing in an unctuous, nasal
tone,
And he looked as if the sermon and the Scriptures
were his own.

But one day the white-haired preacher spoke of
how God's justice fell
Soon or late with awful sureness on the man whose
heart could tell
Of a wrong done to the widow or the orphan, and
he said
That such wrongs were ever living, though the
injured ones were dead.
And old Sculpin's heart was writhing, though his
heavy eyes were closed, —
For, despite his solemn sanctity, at sermon times he
dozed;
But his half-awakened senses heard the preacher
speak of death
And of wrongs done unto orphans, and he dreamed
with wheezing breath

That cold hands were tearing from his heart its
pharisaic screens,
That the preacher was a tiger with the voice of
Nathan Beans!
And he shrieked and jumped up wildly, and upon
the seat stood he,
As if standing on the whaler looking outward on
the sea;
And he clutched as at the rigging with a horror in
his eye,
For he saw the woods of Java and he heard that
human cry,
As he crouched and cowered earthward. And the
simple folk around
Stood with looks of kindly sympathy: they raised
him from the ground,
And they brought him half unconscious to the hum-
ble chapel door,
Whence he fled as from a scourging, and he entered
it no more;
For the sight of that old preacher brought the
horror to his face,

And he dare not meet his neighbors' honest eyes
within the place,
For his conscience like a mirror rose and showed
the dismal scenes,
Where the tiger yelled for ever with the voice of
Nathan Beans.

WESTERN AUSTRALIA.

O BEAUTEOUS Southland! land of yellow air,
That hangeth o'er thee slumbering, and doth hold
The moveless foliage of thy valleys fair
And wooded hills, like aureole of gold.

O thou, discovered ere the fitting time,
Ere Nature in completion turned thee forth!
Ere aught was finished but thy peerless clime,
Thy virgin breath allured the amorous North.

O land, God made thee wondrous to the eye!
But His sweet singers thou hast never heard;
He left thee, meaning to come by-and-bye,
And give rich voice to every bright-winged bird.

He painted with fresh hues thy myriad flowers,
But left them scentless: ah! their woful dole,
Like sad reproach of their Creator's powers,—
To make so sweet fair bodies, void of soul.

He gave thee trees of odorous precious wood;
But, midst them all, bloomed not one tree of fruit.
He looked, but said not that His work was good,
When leaving thee all perfumeless and mute.

He blessed thy flowers with honey: every bell
Looks earthward, sunward, with a yearning wist;
But no bee-lover ever notes the swell
Of hearts, like lips, a-hungering to be kist.

O strange land, thou art virgin! thou art more
Than fig-tree barren! Would that I could paint
For others' eyes the glory of the shore
Where last I saw thee; but the senses faint

In soft delicious dreaming when they drain
  Thy wine of color. Virgin fair thou art,
All sweetly fruitful, waiting with soft pain
  The spouse who comes to wake thy sleeping
    heart.

GOLU.

ONCE I had a little sweetheart
In the land of the Malay, —
Such a little yellow sweetheart!
Warm and peerless as the day
Of her own dear sunny island,
Keimah, in the far, far East,
Where the mango and banana
Made us many a merry feast.

Such a little copper sweetheart
Was my Golu, plump and round,
With her hair all blue-black streaming
O'er her to the very ground.
Soft and clear as dew-drop clinging
To a grass blade was her eye;
For the heart below was purer
Than the hill-stream whispering by.

Costly robes were not for Golu:
  No more raiment did she need
Than the milky budding breadfruit,
  Or the lily of the mead;
And she was my little sweetheart
  Many a sunny summer day,
When we ate the fragrant guavas,
  In the land of the Malay.

Life was laughing then. Ah! Golu,
  Do you think of that old time,
And of all the tales I told you
  Of my colder Western clime?
Do you think how happy were we
  When we sailed to strip the palm,
And we made a latteen arbor
  Of the boat-sail in the calm?

They may call you semi-savage,
  Golu! I cannot forget
How I poised my little sweetheart
  Like a copper statuette.

Now my path lies through the cities;
  But they cannot drive away
My sweet dreams of little Golu
  And the land of the Malay.

CHUNDER ALI'S WIFE.

FROM THE HINDOSTANEE.

"I AM poor," said Chunder Ali, while the Mandarin above him
Frowned in supercilious anger at the dog who dared to speak;
"I am friendless and a Hindoo: such a one meets few to love him
Here in China, where the Hindoo finds the truth alone is weak.
I have naught to buy your justice; were I wise, I had not striven.
Speak your judgment;" and he crossed his arms and bent his quivering face.

Heard he then the unjust sentence: all his goods and gold were given
To another, and he stood alone, a beggar in the place.

And the man who bought the judgment looked in triumph and derision
At the cheated Hindoo merchant, as he rubbed his hands and smiled
At the whispered gratulation of his friends, and at the vision
Of the more than queenly dower for Ahmeer, his only child.
Fair Ahmeer, who of God's creatures was the only one who loved him,
She, the diamond of his treasures, the one lamb within his fold,
She, whose voice, like her dead mother's, was the only power that moved him,—
She would praise the skill that gained her all this Hindoo's silk and gold.
And the old man thanked Confucius, and the judge, and him who pleaded.

But why falls this sudden silence? why does each one hold his breath?
Every eye turns on the Hindoo, who before was all unheeded,
And in wond'ring expectation all the court grows still as death.

Not alone stood Chunder Ali: by his side Ahmeer was standing,
And his brown hand rested lightly on her shoulder as he smiled
At the sweet young face turned toward him. Then the father's voice commanding
Fiercely bade his daughter to him from the dog whose touch defiled.
But she moved not, and she looked not at her father or the others
As she answered, with her eyes upon the Hindoo's noble face:
"Nay, my father, he defiles not: this kind arm above all others
Is my choosing, and forever by his side shall be my place.

When you knew not, his dear hand had given many
a sweet love-token,
He had gathered all my heartstrings and had bound
them round his life;
Yet you tell me he defiles me: nay, my father, you
have spoken
In your anger, and not knowing I was Chunder
Ali's wife."

HIDDEN SINS.

FOR every sin that comes before the light,
And leaves an outward blemish on the soul,
How many, darker, cower out of sight,
And burrow, blind and silent, like the mole.
And like the mole, too, with its busy feet
That dig and dig a never-ending cave,
Our hidden sins gnaw through the soul, and meet
And feast upon each other in its grave.

A buried sin is like a covered sore
That spreads and festers 'neath a painted face;
And no man's art can heal it evermore,
But only His — the Surgeon's — promised grace.
Who hides a sin is like the hunter who
Once warmed a frozen adder with his breath,
And when he placed it near his heart it flew
With poisoned fangs and stung that heart to death.

A sculptor once a granite statue made,
  One-sided only, just to fit its place:
The unseen side was monstrous; so men shade
  Their evil acts behind a smiling face.
O blind! O foolish! thus our sins to hide,
  And force our pleading hearts the gall to sip;
O cowards! who must eat the myrrh, that Pride
  May smile like Virtue with a lying lip.

A sin admitted is nigh half atoned;
  And while the fault is red and freshly done,
If we but drop our eyes and think, — 'tis owned, —
  'Tis half forgiven, half the crown is won.
But if we heedless let it reek and rot,
  Then pile a mountain on its grave, and turn,
With smiles to all the world, — that tainted spot
  Beneath the mound will never cease to burn.

UNSPOKEN WORDS.

THE kindly words that rise within the heart,
  And thrill it with their sympathetic tone,
But die ere spoken, fail to play their part,
  And claim a merit that is not their own.
The kindly word unspoken is a sin, —
  A sin that wraps itself in purest guise,
And tells the heart that, doubting, looks within,
  That not in speech, but thought, the virtue lies.

But 'tis not so: another heart may thirst
  For that kind word, as Hagar in the wild —
Poor banished Hagar! — prayed a well might burst
  From out the sand to save her parching child.
And loving eyes that cannot see the mind
  Will watch the expected movement of the lip:
Ah! can ye let its cutting silence wind
  Around that heart, and scathe it like a whip?

Unspoken words, like treasures in the mine,
  Are valueless until we give them birth:
Like unfound gold their hidden beauties shine,
  Which God has made to bless and gild the earth.
How sad 'twould be to see a master's hand
  Strike glorious notes upon a voiceless lute!
But oh! what pain when, at God's own command,
  A heart-string thrills with kindness, but is mute!

Then hide it not, the music of the soul,
  Dear sympathy, expressed with kindly voice,
But let it like a shining river roll
  To deserts dry, — to hearts that would rejoice.
Oh! let the symphony of kindly words
  Sound for the poor, the friendless, and the weak;
And He will bless you, — He who struck these
    chords
  Will strike another when in turn you seek.

MY NATIVE LAND.

IT chanced to me upon a time to sail
  Across the Southern Ocean to and fro;
And, landing at fair isles, by stream and vale
  Of sensuous blessing did we ofttimes go.
And months of dreamy joys, like joys in sleep,
  Or like a clear, calm stream o'er mossy stone,
Unnoted passed our hearts with voiceless sweep,
  And left us yearning still for lands unknown.

And when we found one, — for 'tis soon to find
  In thousand-isled Cathay another isle, —
For one short noon its treasures filled the mind,
  And then again we yearned, and ceased to smile.
And so it was, from isle to isle we passed,
  Like wanton bees or boys on flowers or lips;

And when that all was tasted, then at last
  We thirsted still for draughts instead of sips.

I learned from this there is no Southern land
  Can fill with love the hearts of Northern men.
Sick minds need change; but, when in health they
    stand
  'Neath foreign skies, their love flies home agen.
And thus with me it was: the yearning turned
  From laden airs of cinnamon away,
And stretched far westward, while the full heart
    burned
  With love for Ireland, looking on Cathay!

My first dear love, all dearer for thy grief!
  My land, that has no peer in all the sea
For verdure, vale, or river, flower or leaf, —
  If first to no man else, thou 'rt first to me.
New loves may come with duties, but the first
  Is deepest yet, — the mother's breath and smiles:
Like that kind face and breast where I was nursed
  Is my poor land, the Niobe of isles.

THE POISON-FLOWER.

IN the evergreen shade of an Austral wood,
Where the long branches laced above,
Through which all day it seemed
The sweet sunbeams down-gleamed
Like the rays of a young mother's love,
When she hides her glad face with her hands and peeps
At the youngling that crows on her knee:
'Neath such ray-shivered shade,
In a banksia glade,
Was this flower first shown to me.

A rich pansy it was, with a small white lip
And a wonderful purple hood;
And your eye caught the sheen
Of its leaves, parrot-green,
Down the dim gothic aisles of the wood.
And its foliage rich on the moistureless sand

Made you long for its odorous breath;
But ah! 'twas to take
To your bosom a snake,
For its pestilent fragrance was death.

And I saw it again, in a far northern land,—
Not a pansy, not purple and white;
Yet in beauteous guise
Did this poison-plant rise,
Fair and fatal again to my sight.
And men longed for her kiss and her odorous breath
When no friend was beside them to tell
That to kiss was to die,
That her truth was a lie,
And her beauty a soul-killing spell.

MY MOTHER'S MEMORY.

THERE is one bright star in heaven
Ever shining in my night;
God to me one guide has given,
Like the sailor's beacon-light,
Set on every shoal and danger,
Sending out its warning ray
To the home-bound weary stranger
Looking for the land-locked bay.

In my farthest, wildest wanderings
I have turned me to that love,
As a diver, 'neath the water,
Turns to watch the light above.

THE OLD SCHOOL CLOCK.

OLD memories rush o'er my mind just now
Of faces and friends of the past;
Of that happy time when life's dream was all bright,
Ere the clear sky of youth was o'ercast.
Very dear are those mem'ries, — they 've clung round my heart,
And bravely withstood Time's rude shock;
But not one is more hallowed or dear to me now
Than the face of the old school clock.

'Twas a quaint old clock with a quaint old face,
And great iron weights and chain;
It stopped when it liked, and before it struck
It creaked as if 'twere in pain.

It had seen many years, and it seemed to say,
  "I 'm one of the real old stock,"
To the youthful fry, who with reverence looked
  On the face of the old school clock.

How many a time have I labored to sketch
  That yellow and time-honored face,
With its basket of flowers, its figures and hands,
  And the weights and the chains in their place!
How oft have I gazed with admiring eye,
  As I sat on the wooden block,
And pondered and guessed at the wonderful things
  That were inside that old school clock!

What a terrible frown did the old clock wear
  To the truant, who timidly cast
An anxious eye on those merciless hands,
  That for him had been moving too fast!
But its frown soon changed; for it loved to smile
  On the thoughtless, noisy flock,
And it creaked and whirred and struck with glee,—
  Did that genial, good-humored old clock.

Well, years had passed, and my mind was filled
  With the world, its cares and ways,
When again I stood in that little school
  Where I passed my boyhood's days.
My old friend was gone! and there hung a thing
  That my sorrow seemed to mock,
As I gazed with a tear and a softened heart
  At a new-fashioned Yankee clock.

'Twas a gaudy thing with bright painted sides,
  And it looked with insolent stare
On the desks and the seats and on every thing old;
  And I thought of the friendly air
Of the face that I missed, with its weights and chains, —
  All gone to the auctioneer's block:
'Tis a thing of the past, — never more shall I see
  But in memory that old school clock.

'Tis the way of the world: old friends pass away,
  And fresh faces arise in their stead;
But still 'mid the din and the bustle of life
  We cherish fond thoughts of the dead.

Yes, dear are those mem'ries: they 've clung round
my heart,
And bravely withstood Time's rude shock;
But not one is more hallowed or dear to me now
Than the face of that old school clock.

A LEGEND OF THE BLESSED VIRGIN.

[The legend is taken from an old miracle-play of the fifteenth century, a reference to which is to be found in Rev. Mr. Hudson's late excellent book on Shakespeare's Times and Characters. The author had turned the legend into verse before he perceived that it differed essentially from the Scripture narrative, its antiquity misleading him.]

THE day of Joseph's marriage unto Mary,
In thoughtful mood he said unto his wife,
"Behold, I go into a far-off country
To labor for thee, and to make thy life
And home all sweet and peaceful." And the Virgin
Unquestioning beheld her spouse depart:
Then lived she many days of musing gladness,
Not knowing that God's hand was round her heart.

And dreaming thus one day within her chamber,
She wept with speechless bliss, when lo! the face
Of white-winged angel Gabriel rose before her,
And bowing spoke, "Hail! Mary, full of grace,

The Lord is with thee, and among the nations
Forever blessed is thy chosen name."
The angel vanished, and the Lord's high Presence
With untold glory to the Virgin came.

A season passed of joy unknown to mortals,
When Joseph came with what his toil had won,
And broke the brooding ecstasy of Mary,
Whose soul was ever with her promised Son.
But nature's jealous fears encircled Joseph,
And round his heart in darkening doubts held sway.
He looked upon his spouse cold-eyed, and pondered
How he could put her from his sight away.

And once, when moody thus within his garden,
The gentle girl besought for some ripe fruit
That hung beyond her reach, the old man answered,
With face averted, harshly to her suit:
"I will not serve thee, woman! Thou hast wronged me:

I heed no more thy words and actions mild;
If fruit thou wantest, thou canst henceforth ask it
From him, the father of thy unborn child!"

But ere the words had root within her hearing,
The Virgin's face was glorified anew;
And Joseph, turning, sank within her presence,
And knew indeed his wondrous dreams were true.
For there before the sandalled feet of Mary
The kingly tree had bowed its top, and she
Had pulled and eaten from its prostrate branches,
As if unconscious of the mystery.

THE WRECK OF THE ATLANTIC.

FOR months and years, with penury and want
  And heart-sore envy did they dare to cope ;
And mite by mite was saved from earnings scant,
  To buy, some future day, the God-sent hope.

They trod the crowded streets of hoary towns,
  Or tilled from year to year the wearied fields,
And in the shadow of the golden crowns
  They gasped for sunshine and the health it yields.

They turned from homes all cheerless, child and man,
  With kindly feelings only for the soil,
And for the kindred faces, pinched and wan,
  That prayed, and stayed, unwilling, at their toil.

They lifted up their faces to the Lord,
  And read His answer in the westering sun
That called them ever as a shining word,
  And beckoned seaward as the rivers run.

They looked their last, wet-eyed, on Swedish
hills,
On German villages and English dales;
Like brooks that grow from many mountain rills
The peasant-stream flowed out from Irish vales.

Their grief at parting was not all a grief,
But blended sweetly with the joy to come,
When from full store they spared the rich relief
To gladden all the dear ones left at home.

"We thank thee, God!" they cried; "the cruel
gate
That barred our lives has swung beneath Thy
hand;
Behind our ship now frowns the cruel fate,
Before her smiles the teeming Promised Land!"

. . . . .

Alas! when shown in mercy or in wrath,
How weak we are to read God's awful lore!
His breath protected on the stormy path,
And dashed them lifeless on the promised
shore!

His hand sustained them in the parting woe,
  And gave bright vision to the heart of each;
His waters bore them where they wished to go,
  Then swept them seaward from the very beach!

Their home is reached, their fetters now are riven,
  Their humble toil is o'er, — their rest has come;
A land was promised and a land is given, —
  But, oh! God help the waiting ones at home!

WITHERED SNOWDROPS.

THEY came in the early spring-days,
With the first refreshing showers;
And I watched the growing beauty
Of the little drooping flowers.

They had no bright hues to charm me,
No gay painting to allure;
But they made me think of angels,
They were all so white and pure.

In the early morns I saw them,
Dew-drops clinging to each bell,
And the first glad sunbeam hasting
Just to kiss them ere they fell.

Daily grew their spotless beauty;
But I feared when chill winds blew

They were all too frail and tender,—
  And alas! my fears were true.

One glad morn I went to see them
  While the bright drops gemmed their snow,
And one angel flower was withered,
  Its fair petals drooping low.

Its white sister's tears fell on it,
  And the sunbeam sadly shone;
For its innocence was withered,
  And its purity was gone.

Still I left it there: I could not
  Tear it rudely from its place;
It might rise again, and summer
  Might restore its vanished grace.

But my hopes grew weaker, weaker,
  And my heart with grief was pained
When I knew it must be severed
  From the innocence it stained.

I must take it from the pure ones:
  Henceforth they must live apart.
But I could not cut my flow'ret —
  My lost angel — from my heart.

Oft I think of that dead snowdrop,
  Think with sorrow, when I meet,
Day by day, the poor lost flowers, —
  Sullied snowdrops of the street.

They were pure once, loved and loving,
  And there still lives good within.
Ah! speak gently to them: harsh words
  Will not lead them from their sin.

The are not like withered flowers
  That can never bloom again:
They can rise, bright angel snowdrops,
  Purified from every stain.

THE WAIL OF TWO CITIES.

CHICAGO, OCTOBER 9, 1871.

GAUNT in the midst of the prairie,
She who was once so fair;
Charred and rent are her garments,
Heavy and dark like cerements;
Silent, but round her the air
Plaintively wails, "Miserere!"

Proud like a beautiful maiden,
Art-like from forehead to feet,
Was she till pressed like a leman
Close to the breast of the demon,
Lusting for one so sweet,
So were her shoulders laden.

Friends she had, rich in her treasures:
Shall the old taunt be true,—
Fallen, they turn their cold faces,
Seeking new wealth-gilded places,
Saying we never knew
Aught of her smiles or her pleasures?

Silent she stands on the prairie,
Wrapped in her fire-scathed sheet:
Around her, thank God! is the Nation,
Weeping for her desolation,
Pouring its gold at her feet,
Answering her "Miserere!"

BOSTON, NOVEMBER 9, 1872.

O broad-breasted Queen among Nations!
O Mother, so strong in thy youth!
Has the Lord looked upon thee in ire,
And willed thou be chastened by fire,
Without any ruth?

Has the Merciful tired of His mercy,
And turned from thy sinning in wrath,
That the world with raised hands sees and pities
Thy desolate daughters, thy cities,
Despoiled on their path?

One year since thy youngest was stricken:
Thy eldest lies stricken to-day.
Ah! God, was thy wrath without pity,
To tear the strong heart from our city,
And cast it away?

O Father! forgive us our doubting;
The stain from our weak souls efface;
Thou rebukest, we know, but to chasten;
Thy hand has but fallen to hasten
Return to thy grace.

Let us rise purified from our ashes
As sinners have risen who grieved;
Let us show that twice-sent desolation
On every true heart in the nation
Has conquest achieved.

THE FISHERMEN OF WEXFORD.

THERE is an old tradition sacred held in Wexford town,
That says: "Upon St. Martin's eve no net shall be let down;
No fishermen of Wexford shall, upon that holy day,
Set sail or cast a line within the scope of Wexford Bay."
The tongue that framed the order, or the time, no one could tell;
And no one ever questioned, but the people kept it well.
And never in man's memory was fisher known to leave
The little town of Wexford on the good St. Martin's Eve.

Alas! alas for Wexford! once upon that holy
day
Came a wondrous shoal of herring to the waters of
the Bay.
The fishers and their families stood out upon the
beach,
And all day watched with wistful eyes the wealth
they might not reach.
Such shoal was never seen before, and keen regrets
went round—
Alas! alas for Wexford! Hark! what is that
grating sound?
The boats' keels on the shingle! Mothers! wives!
ye well may grieve,—
The fishermen of Wexford mean to sail on Martin's
Eve!

"Oh, stay ye!" cried the women wild. "Stay!"
cried the men white-haired;
"And dare ye not to do this thing your fathers
never dared.

No man can thrive who tempts the Lord!"
"Away!" they cried: "the Lord
Ne'er sent a shoal of fish but as a fisherman's reward."
And scoffingly they said, "To-night our nets shall sweep the Bay,
And take the Saint who guards it, should he come across our way!"
The keels have touched the water, and the crews are in each boat;
And on St. Martin's Eve the Wexford fishers are afloat!

The moon is shining coldly on the sea and on the land,
On dark faces in the fishing-fleet and pale ones on the strand,
As seaward go the daring boats, and heavenward the cries
Of kneeling wives and mothers with uplifted hands and eyes.

"O Holy Virgin! be their guard!" the weeping
women cried;
The old men, sad and silent, watched the boats
cleave through the tide,
As past the farthest headland, past the lighthouse,
in a line
The fishing-fleet went seaward through the phos-
phor-lighted brine.

Oh, pray, ye wives and mothers! All your prayers
they sorely need
To save them from the wrath they 've roused by
their rebellious greed.
Oh! white-haired men and little babes, and weep-
ing sweethearts, pray
To God to spare the fishermen to-night in Wexford
Bay!

The boats have reached good offing, and, as out the
nets are thrown,
The hearts ashore are chilled to hear the soughing
sea wind's moan:

Like to a human heart that loved, and hoped for
some return,
To find at last but hatred, so the sea-wind seemed
to mourn.
But ah! the Wexford fishermen! their nets did
scarcely sink
One inch below the foam, when, lo! the daring
boatmen shrink
With sudden awe and whitened lips and glaring
eyes agape,
For breast-high, threatening, from the sea uprose a
Human Shape!

Beyond them, — in the moonlight, — hand upraised
and awful mien,
Waving back and pointing landwards, breast-high
in the sea 'twas seen.
Thrice it waved and thrice it pointed, — then, with
clenchéd hand upraised,
The awful shape went down before the fishers as
they gazed!

Gleaming whitely through the water, fathoms deep
they saw its frown,—
They saw its white hand clenched above it,—sink-
ing slowly down!
And then there was a rushing 'neath the boats, and
every soul
Was thrilled with greed: they knew it was the
seaward-going shoal!

Defying the dread warning, every face was sternly
set,
And wildly did they ply the oar, and wildly haul
the net.
But two boats' crews obeyed the sign,—God-fearing
men were they,—
They cut their lines and left their nets, and home-
ward sped away;
But darkly rising sternwards did God's wrath in
tempest sweep,
And they, of all the fishermen, that night escaped
the deep.

Oh, wives and mothers, sweethearts, sires! well
might ye mourn next day;
For seventy fishers' corpses strewed the shores of
Wexford Bay!

THE FLYING DUTCHMAN.

LONG time ago, from Amsterdam a vessel sailed away, —
As fair a ship as ever flung aside the laughing spray.
Upon the shore were tearful eyes, and scarfs were in the air,
As to her, o'er the Zuyder Zee, went fond adieu and prayer;
And brave hearts, yearning shoreward from the outward-going ship,
Felt lingering kisses clinging still to tear-wet cheek and lip.
She steered for some far eastern clime, and, as she skimmed the seas,
Each taper mast was bending like a rod before the breeze.

Her captain was a stalwart man, — an iron heart
had he, —
From childhood's days he sailed upon the rolling
Zuyder Zee:
He nothing feared upon the earth, and scarcely
heaven feared,
He would have dared and done whatever mortal
man had dared!
He looked aloft, where high in air the pennant cut
the blue,
And every rope and spar and sail was firm and
strong and true.
He turned him from the swelling sail to gaze upon
the shore, —
Ah! little thought the skipper then 'twould meet
his eye no more:
He dreamt not that an awful doom was hanging
o'er his ship,
That Vanderdecken's name would yet make pale
the speaker's lip.
The vessel bounded on her way, and spire and
dome went down, —

Ere darkness fell, beneath the wave had sunk the
distant town.
No more, no more, ye hapless crew, shall Holland
meet your eye.
In lingering hope and keen suspense, maid, wife,
and child shall die!

Away, away the vessel speeds, till sea and sky
alone
Are round her, as her course she steers across the
torrid zone.
Away, until the North Star fades, the Southern
Cross is high,
And myriad gems of brightest beam are sparkling
in the sky.
The tropic winds are left behind; she nears the
Cape of Storms,
Where awful Tempest ever sits enthroned in wild
alarms;
Where Ocean in his anger shakes aloft his foamy
crest,
Disdainful of the weakly toys that ride upon his
breast.

Fierce swell the winds and waters round the Dutch-
man's gallant ship,
But, to their rage, defiance rings from Vander-
decken's lip :
Impotent they to make him swerve, their might he
dares despise,
As straight he holds his onward course, and wind
and wave defies.
For days and nights he struggles in the wierd,
unearthly fight.
His brow is bent, his eye is fierce, but looks of deep
affright
Amongst the mariners go round, as hopelessly they
steer :
They do not dare to murmur, but they whisper
what they fear.
Their black-browed captain awes them : 'neath his
darkened eye they quail,
And in a grim and sullen mood their bitter fate
bewail.
As some fierce rider ruthless spurs a timid, wav-
ering horse,

He drives his shapely vessel, and they watch the
reckless course,
Till once again their skipper's laugh is flung upon
the blast:
The placid ocean smiles beyond, the dreaded Cape
is passed!

Away across the Indian main the vessel northward
glides;
A thousand murmuring ripples break along her
graceful sides:
The perfumed breezes fill her sails, — her destined
port she nears, —
The captain's brow has lost its frown, the mariners
their fears.
"Land ho!" at length the welcome sound the
watchful sailor sings,
And soon within an Indian bay the ship at anchor
swings.
Not idle then the busy crew: ere long the spacious
hold
Is emptied of its western freight, and stored with
silk and gold.

Again the ponderous anchor 's weighed; the shore
is left behind,
The snowy sails are bosomed out before the favoring wind.
Across the warm blue Indian sea the vessel southward flies,
And once again the North Star fades and Austral
beacons rise.
For home she steers! she seems to know and
answer to the word,
And swifter skims the burnished deep, like some
fair ocean-bird.
"For home! for home!" the merry crew with
gladsome voices cry,
And dark-browed Vanderdecken has a mild light
in his eye.

But once again the Cape draws near, and furious
billows rise;
And still the daring Dutchman's laugh the hurricane defies.
But wildly shrieked the tempest ere the scornful
sound had died,

A warning to the daring man to curb his impious
pride.
A crested mountain struck the ship, and like a
frighted bird
She trembled 'neath the awful shock. Then Van-
derdecken heard
A pleading voice within the gale, — his better an-
gel spoke,
But fled before his scowling look, as mast-high
mountains broke
Around the trembling vessel, till the crew with
terror paled;
But Vanderdecken never flinched, nor 'neath the
thunders quailed.
With folded arms and stern-pressed lips, dark anger
in his eye,
He answered back the threatening frown that
lowered o'er the sky.
With fierce defiance in his heart, and scornful look
of flame,
He spoke, and thus with impious voice blasphemed
God's holy name: —

"Howl on, ye winds! ye tempests, howl! your rage is spent in vain:
Despite your strength, your frowns, your hate, I 'll ride upon the main.
Defiance to your idle shrieks! I 'll sail upon my path:
I cringe not for thy Maker's smile, — I care not for His wrath!"

He ceased. An awful silence fell: the tempest and the sea
Were hushed in sudden stillness by the Ruler's dread decree.
The ship was riding motionless within the gathering gloom;
The Dutchman stood upon the poop and heard his dreadful doom.
The hapless crew were on the deck in swooning terror prone, —
They, too, were bound in fearful fate. In angered thunder-tone

The judgment words swept o'er the sea: "Go, wretch, accurst, condemned!
Go sail for ever on the deep, by shrieking tempests hemmed.
No home, no port, no calm, no rest, no gentle fav'ring breeze,
Shall ever greet thee. Go, accurst! and battle with the seas!
Go, braggart! struggle with the storm, nor ever cease to live,
But bear a million times the pangs that death and fear can give.
Away! and hide thy guilty head, a curse to all thy kind
Who ever see thee struggling, wretch, with ocean and with wind.
Away, presumptuous worm of earth! Go teach thy fellow-worms
The awful fate that waits on him who braves the King of Storms!"

'Twas o'er. A lurid lightning flash lit up the sea and sky
Around and o'er the fated ship; then rose a wailing cry
From every heart within her, of keen anguish and despair;
But mercy was for them no more, — it died away in air.

Once more the lurid light gleamed out, — the ship was still at rest,
The crew were standing at their posts; with arms across his breast
Still stood the captain on the poop, but bent and crouching now
He bowed beneath that fiat dread, and o'er his swarthy brow
Swept lines of anguish, as if he a thousand years of pain
Had lived and suffered. Then across the heaving, angry main

The tempest shrieked triumphant, and the angry
waters hissed
Their vengeful hate against the toy they oftentimes
had kissed.
And ever through the midnight storm that hapless
crew must speed:
They try to round the stormy Cape, but never can
succeed.
And oft when gales are wildest, and the lightning's
vivid sheen
Flashes back the ocean's anger, still the Phantom
Ship is seen
Ever sailing to the southward in the fierce tor-
nado's swoop,
With her ghostly crew and canvas, and her captain
on the poop,
Unrelenting, unforgiven; and 'tis said that every
word
Of his blasphemous defiance still upon the gale is
heard!
But Heaven help the ship near which the dismal
sailor steers, —

The doom of those is sealed to whom that Phantom Ship appears:
They 'll never reach their destined port, — they 'll see their homes no more, —
They who see the Flying Dutchman — never, never reach the shore!

UNCLE NED'S TALE.

AN OLD DRAGOON'S STORY.

I OFTEN, musing, wander back to days long since gone by,
And far-off scenes and long-lost forms arise to fancy's eye.
A group familiar now I see, who all but one are fled, —
My mother, sister Jane, myself, and dear old Uncle Ned.
I 'll tell you how I see them now. First, mother in her chair
Sits knitting by the parlor fire, with anxious matron air;
My sister Jane, just nine years old, is seated at her feet,
With look demure, as if she, too, were thinking how to meet

The butcher's or the baker's bill, — though not a thought has she
Of aught beside her girlish toys; and next to her I see
Myself, a sturdy lad of twelve, — neglectful of the book
That open lies upon my knee, — my fixed admiring look
At Uncle Ned, upon the left, whose upright, martial mien,
Whose empty sleeve and gray moustache, proclaim what he has been.
My mother I had always loved; my father then was dead;
But 'twas more than love — 'twas worship — I felt for Uncle Ned.
Such tales he had of battle-fields, — the victory and the rout,
The ringing cheer, the dying shriek, the loud exulting shout!
And how, forgetting age and wounds, his eye would kindle bright,

When telling of some desperate ride or close and deadly fight!
But oft I noticed, in the midst of some wild martial tale,
To which I lent attentive ear, my mother's cheek grow pale:
She sighed to see my kindled look, and feared I might be led
To follow in the wayward steps of poor old Uncle Ned.
But with all the wondrous tales he told, 'twas strange I never heard
Of his last fight, for of that day he never spoke a word.
And yet 'twas there he lost his arm, and once he e'en confessed
'Twas there he won the glittering cross he wore upon his breast.
It hung the centre of a group of Glory's emblems fair,
And royal hands, he told me once, had placed the bauble there.

Each day that passed I hungered more to hear about that fight,
And oftentimes I prayed in vain. At length, one winter's night, —
The very night I speak of now, — with more than usual care
I filled his pipe, then took my stand beside my uncle's chair:
I fixed my eyes upon the Cross, — he saw my youthful plan;
And, smiling, laid the pipe aside and thus the tale began: —

"Well, boy, it was in summer time, and just at morning's light
We heard the 'Boot and Saddle!' sound: the foe was then in sight,
Just winding round a distant hill and opening on the plain.
Each trooper looked with careful eye to girth and curb and rein.

We snatched a hasty breakfast, — we were old
campaigners then:
That morn, of all our splendid corps, we 'd scarce
one hundred men;
But they were soldiers, tried and true, who 'd
rather die than yield:
The rest were scattered far and wide o'er many a
hard-fought field.
Our trumpet now rang sharply out, and at a
swinging pace
We left the bivouac behind; and soon the eye
could trace
The columns moving o'er the plain. Oh! 'twas a
stirring sight
To see two mighty armies there preparing for the
fight:
To watch the heavy masses, as, with practised,
steady wheel,
They opened out in slender lines of brightly flash-
ing steel.
Our place was on the farther flank, behind some
rising ground,

That hid the stirring scene from view; but soon a
booming sound
Proclaimed the opening of the fight. Then war's
loud thunder rolled,
And hurtling shells and whistling balls their deadly
message told.
We hoped to have a gallant day; our hearts were
all aglow;
We longed for one wild, sweeping charge, to chase
the flying foe.
Our troopers marked the hours glide by, but still
no orders came:
They clutched their swords, and muttered words
'twere better not to name.
For hours the loud artillery roared, — the sun was
at its height, —
Still there we lay behind that hill, shut out from
all the fight!
We heard the maddened charging yells, the ringing
British cheers,
And all the din of glorious war kept sounding in
our ears.

Our hearts with fierce impatience throbbed, we cursed the very hill
That hid the sight: the evening fell, and we were idle still.
The horses, too, were almost wild, and told with angry snort
And blazing eye their fierce desire to join the savage sport.
When lower still the sun had sunk, and with it all our hope,
A horseman, soiled with smoke and sweat, came dashing down the slope.
He bore the wished-for orders. 'At last!' our Colonel cried;
And as he read the brief despatch his glance was filled with pride.
Then he who bore the orders, in a low, emphatic tone,
The stern, expressive sentence spoke,—'*He said it must be done!*'
'It *shall* be done!' our Colonel cried. 'Men, look to strap and girth,

We 've work to do this day will prove what every
man is worth;
Ay, work, my lads, will make amends for all our
long delay,—
The General says on us depends the fortune of the
day!'

"No order needed we to mount,—each man was
in his place,
And stern and dangerous was the look on every
veteran face.
We trotted sharply up the hill, and halted on the
brow,
And then that glorious field appeared. Oh! lad,
I see it now!
But little time had we to spare for idle gazing then:
Beneath us, in the valley, stood a dark-clad mass of
men:
It cut the British line in two. Our Colonel shouted,
'There!
Behold your work! Our orders are *to charge and
break that square!*'

Each trooper drew a heavy breath, then gathered
up his reins,
And pressed the helmet o'er his brow; the horses
tossed their manes
In protest fierce against the curb, and spurned the
springy heath,
Impatient for the trumpet's sound to bid them rush
to death.

"Well, boy, that moment seemed an hour: at last
we heard the words, —
'Dragoons! I know you 'll follow me. Ride steady,
men! Draw swords!'
The trumpet sounded: off we dashed, at first with
steady pace,
But growing swifter as we went. Oh! 'twas a
gallant race!
Three-fourths the ground was left behind: the loud
and thrilling 'Charge!'
Rang out; but, fairly frantic now, we needed not
to urge

With voice or rein our gallant steeds, or touch
their foaming flanks.
They seemed to fly. Now straight in front appeared
the kneeling ranks.
Above them waved a standard broad: we saw their
rifles raised, —
A moment more, with awful crash, the deadly
volley blazed.
The bullets whistled through our ranks, and many
a trooper fell;
But we were left. What cared we then? but on-
ward rushing still!
Again the crash roared fiercely out; but on! still
madly on!
We heard the shrieks of dying men, but recked not
who was gone.
We gored the horses' foaming flanks, and on through
smoke and glare
We wildly dashed, with clenchéd teeth. We had
no thought, no care!
Then came a sudden, sweeping rush. Again with
savage heel

I struck my horse: with awful bound he rose right
o'er their steel!

"Well, boy, I cannot tell you how that dreadful
leap was made,
But there I rode, inside the square, and grasped a
reeking blade.
I cared not that I was alone, my eyes seem filled
with blood:
I never thought a man could feel in such a mur-
derous mood.
I parried not, nor guarded thrusts; I felt not pain
or wound,
But madly spurred the frantic horse, and swept my
sword around.
I tried to reach the standard sheet; but there at
last was foiled.
The gallant horse was jaded now, and from the
steel recoiled.
They saw his fright, and pressed him then: his
terror made him rear,
And falling back he crushed their ranks, and broke
their guarded square!

My comrades saw the gap he made, and soon came
dashing in;
They raised me up, — I felt no hurt, but mingled
in the din.
I 'd seen some fearful work before, but never was
engaged
In such a wild and savage fight as now around me
raged.
The foe had ceased their firing, and now plied the
deadly steel:
Though all our men were wounded then, no pain
they seemed to feel.
No groans escaped from those who fell, but horrid
oaths instead,
And scowling looks of hate were on the features
of the dead.
The fight was round the standard: though outnum-
bered ten to one,
We held our ground, — ay, more than that, — we
still kept pushing on.
Our men now made a desperate rush to take the
flag by storm.

I seized the pole, a blow came down and crushed
my outstretched arm.
I felt a sudden thrill of pain, but that soon passed
away;
And, with a devilish thirst for blood, again I joined
the fray.
At last we rallied all our strength, and charged o'er
heaps of slain:
Some fought to death; some wavered, — then fled
across the plain.

"Well, boy, the rest is all confused: there was a
fearful rout;
I saw our troopers chase the foe, and heard their
maddened shout.
Then came a blank: my senses reeled, I know not
how I fell;
I seemed to grapple with a foe, but that I cannot
tell.
My mind was gone: when it came back I saw the
moon on high;
Around me all was still as death. I gazed up at
the sky,

And watched the glimmering stars above, — so
quiet did they seem, —
And all that dreadful field appeared like some wild,
fearful dream.
But memory soon came back again, and cleared my
wandering brain,
And then from every joint and limb shot fiery darts
of pain.
My throat was parched, the burning thirst increased
with every breath;
I made no effort to arise, but wished and prayed for
death.
My bridle arm was broken, and lay throbbing on
the sward,
But something still my right hand grasped: I
thought it was my sword.
I raised my hand to cast it off, — no reeking blade
was there;
Then life and strength returned, — I held the
Standard of the Square!
With bounding heart I gained my feet. Oh! then
I wished to live,

'Twas strange the strength and love of life that
standard seemed to give!
I gazed around: far down the vale I saw a camp-
fire's glow.
With wandering step I ran that way, — I recked
not friend or foe.
Though stumbling now o'er heaps of dead, now
o'er a stiffened horse,
I heeded not, but watched the light, and held my
onward course.
But soon that flash of strength had failed, and
checked my feverish speed;
Again my throat was all ablaze, my wounds began
to bleed.
I knew that if I fell again, my chance of life was
gone,
So, leaning on the standard-pole, I still kept strug-
gling on.
At length I neared the camp-fire: there were scar-
let jackets round,
And swords and brazen helmets lay strewn upon
the ground.

Some distance off, in order ranged, stood men, — about a score:
O God! 'twas all that now remained of my old gallant corps!
The muster-roll was being called: to every well-known name
I heard the solemn answer, — 'Dead!' At length my own turn came.
I paused to hear, — a comrade answered, 'Dead! I saw him fall!'
I could not move another step, I tried in vain to call.
My life was flowing fast, and all around was gathering haze,
And o'er the heather tops I watched my comrades' cheerful blaze.
I thought such anguish as I felt was more than man could bear.
O God! it was an awful thing to die with help so near!
And death was stealing o'er me: with the strength of wild despair
I raised the standard o'er my head, and waved it through the air.

Then all grew dim: the fire, the men, all vanished
from my sight,
My senses reeled; I know no more of that eventful
night.
'Twas weeks before my mind came back: I knew
not where I lay,
But kindly hands were round me, and old comrades
came each day.
They told me how the waving flag that night had
caught their eye,
And how they found me bleeding there, and thought
that I must die;
They brought me all the cheering news, — the war
was at an end.
No wonder 'twas, with all their care, I soon began
to mend.
The General came to see me, too, with all his bril-
liant train,
But what he said, or how I felt, to tell you now
'twere vain.
Enough, I soon grew strong again: the wished-for
route had come,

And all the gallant veteran troops set out with cheers for home.
We soon arrived; and then, my lad, 'twould thrill your heart to hear
How England welcomed home her sons with many a ringing cheer.
But tush! what boots it now to speak of what was said or done?
The victory was dearly bought, our bravest hearts were gone.
Ere long the King reviewed us. Ah! that memory is sweet!
They made me bear the foreign flag, and lay it at his feet.
I parted from my brave old corps: 'twere matter, lad, for tears,
To leave the kind old comrades I had ridden with for years.
I was no longer fit for war, my wanderings had to cease.
There, boy, I 've told you all my tales. Now let me smoke in peace."

How vivid grows the picture now! how bright
each scene appears!
I trace each loved and long-lost face with eyes be-
dimmed in tears.
How plain I hear thee, Uncle Ned, and see thy
musing look,
Comparing all thy glory to the curling wreaths of
smoke!
A truer, braver soldier ne'er for king and country
bled.
His wanderings are for ever o'er. God rest thee,
Uncle Ned!

UNCLE NED'S TALES.

HOW THE FLAG WAS SAVED.*

'TWAS a dismal winter's evening, fast without
came down the snow,
But within, the cheerful fire cast a ruddy, genial
glow
O'er our pleasant little parlor, that was then my
mother's pride.
There she sat beside the glowing grate, my sister
by her side;
And beyond, within the shadow, in a cosy little
nook
Uncle Ned and I were sitting, and in whispering
tones we spoke.
I was asking for a story he had promised me to
tell,—

* An incident from the record of the Enniskillen Dragoons in Spain, under General Picton.

Of his comrade, old Dick Hilton, how he fought and how he fell;
And with eager voice I pressed him, till a mighty final cloud
Blew he slowly, then upon his breast his grisly head he bowed,
And, musing, stroked his gray mustache ere he began to speak,
Then brushed a tear that stole along his bronzed and furrowed cheek.
"Ah, no! I will not speak to-night of that sad tale," he cried:
"Some other time I'll tell you, boy, about that splendid ride.
Your words have set me thinking of the many careless years
That comrade rode beside me, and have caused these bitter tears;
For I loved him, boy, — for twenty years we galloped rein to rein, —
In peace and war, through all that time, stanch comrades had we been.

As boys we rode together when our soldiering first
began,
And in all those years I knew him for a true and
trusty man.
One who never swerved from danger, — for he knew
not how to fear, —
If grim Death arrayed his legions, Dick would
charge him with a cheer.
He was happiest in a struggle or a wild and dangerous ride:
Every inch a trooper was he, and he cared for
naught beside.
He was known for many a gallant deed: to-night
I 'll tell you one,
And no braver feat of arms was by a soldier ever
done.
'Twas when we were young and fearless, for 'twas
in our first campaign,
When we galloped through the orange groves and
fields of sunny Spain.
Our wary old commander was retiring from the
foe,

Who came pressing close upon us, with a proud,
exulting show.
We could hear their taunting laughter, and within
our very sight
Did they ride defiant round us,—ay, and dared us
to the fight.
But brave old Picton heeded not, but held his
backward track,
And smiling said the day would come to pay the
Frenchmen back.
And come it did: one morning, long before the
break of day,
We were standing to our arms, all ready for the
coming fray.
Soon the sun poured down his glory on the hostile
lines arrayed,
And his beams went flashing brightly back from
many a burnished blade,
Soon to change its spotless lustre for a reeking
crimson stain,
In some heart, then throbbing proudly, that will
never throb again

When that sun has reached his zenith, life and
pride will then have fled,
And his beams will mock in splendor o'er the
ghastly heaps of dead.
Oh, 'tis sad to think how many —— but I wander,
lad, I fear;
And, though the moral 's good, I guess the tale
you 'd rather hear.
Well, I said that we were ready, and the foe was
ready, too;
Soon the fight was raging fiercely, — thick and fast
the bullets flew,
With a bitter hiss of malice, as if hungry for the
life
To be torn from manly bosoms in the maddening
heat of strife.
Distant batteries were thundering, pouring grape
and shell like rain,
And the cruel missiles hurtled with their load of
death and pain,
Which they carried, like fell demons, to the heart
of some brigade,

Where the sudden, awful stillness told the havoc
they had made.
Thus the struggle raged till noon, and neither side
could vantage show;
Then the tide of battle turned, and swept in favor
of the foe!
Fiercer still the cannon thundered, — wilder
screamed the grape and shell, —
Onward pressed the French battalions, — back the
British masses fell!
Then, as on its prey devoted, fierce the hungered
vulture swoops,
Swung the foeman's charging squadrons down upon
our broken troops.
Victory hovered o'er their standard, — on they
swept with maddened shout,
Spreading death and havoc round them, till retreat
was changed to rout!
'Twas a saddening sight to witness; and, when
Picton saw them fly,
Grief and shame were mixed and burning in the
old commander's eye.

We were riding in his escort, close behind him, on a height
Which the fatal field commanded; thence we viewed the growing flight.

"But, my lad, I now must tell you something more about that hill,
And I'll try to make you see the spot as I can see it still.
Right before us, o'er the battle-field, the fall was sheer and steep;
On our left the ground fell sloping, in a pleasant, grassy sweep,
Where the aides went dashing swiftly, bearing orders to and fro,
For by that sloping side alone they reached the plain below.
On our right — now pay attention, boy — a yawning fissure lay,
As if an earthquake's shock had split the mountain's side away.
And in the dismal gulf, far down, we heard the angry roar

Of a foaming mountain torrent, that, mayhap, the
cleft had wore,
As it rushed for countless ages through its black
and secret lair;
But no matter how 'twas formed, my lad, the
yawning gulf was there.
And from the farther side a stone projected o'er the
gorge, —
'Twas strange to see the massive rock just balanced
on the verge;
It seemed as if an eagle's weight the ponderous
mass of stone
Would topple from its giddy height, and send it
crashing down.
It stretched far o'er the dark abyss; but, though
'twere footing good,
'Twas twenty feet or more from off the side on
which we stood.
Beyond the cleft a gentle slope went down and
joined the plain, —
Now, lad, back to where we halted, and again
resume the rein.

I said our troops were routed. Far and near they
broke and fled,
The grape-shot tearing through them, leaving lanes
of mangled dead.
All order lost, they left the fight, — they threw
their arms away,
And joined in one wild panic rout, — ah! 'twas a
bitter day!

"But did I say that *all* was lost? Nay, one brave
corps stood fast,
Determined they would never fly, but fight it to
the last.
They barred the Frenchman from his prey, and
his whole fury braved, —
One brief hour could they hold their ground, the
army might be saved.
Fresh troops were hurrying to our aid, — we saw
their glittering head, —
Ah, God! how those brave hearts were raked by
the death-shower of lead!
But stand they did: they never flinched nor took
one backward stride,

They sent their bayonets home, and then with
stubborn courage died.
But few were left of that brave band when the
dread hour had passed,
Still, faint and few, they held their flag above them
to the last.
But now a cloud of horsemen, like a shadowy
avalanche,
Sweeps down: as Picton sees them, e'en his cheek
is seen to blanch.
They were not awed, that little band, but rallied
once again,
And sent us back a farewell cheer. Then burst
from reckless men
The anguished cry, 'God help them!' as we saw
the feeble flash
Of their last defiant volley, when upon them with
a crash
Burst the gleaming lines of riders, — one by one
they disappear,
And the chargers' hoofs are trampling on the last
of that brave square!

On swept the squadrons! Then we looked where
last the band was seen:
A scarlet heap was all that marked the place where
they had been!
Still forward spurred the horsemen, eager to complete the rout;
But our lines had been re-formed now, and five
thousand guns belched out
A reception to the squadrons,—rank on rank was
piled that day,
Every bullet hissed out 'Vengeance!' as it whistled on its way.

"And now it was, with maddened hearts, we saw
a galling sight:
A French hussar was riding close beneath us on
the right,—
He held a British standard! With insulting shout
he stood,
And waved the flag,—its heavy folds drooped
down with shame and blood,—
The blood of hearts unconquered: 'twas the flag
of the stanch corps

That had fought to death beneath it, — it was heavy
with their gore.
The foreign dog! I see him as he holds the
standard down,
And makes his charger trample on its colors and
its crown!
But his life soon paid the forfeit: with a cry of
rage and pain,
Hilton dashes from the escort, like a tiger from his
chain.
Nought he sees but that insulter; and he strikes
his frightened horse
With his clenchéd hand, and spurs him, with a
bitter-spoken curse,
Straight as bullet from a rifle — but, great Lord!
he has not seen,
In his angry thirst for vengeance, the black gulf
that lies between!
All our warning shouts unheeded, starkly on he
headlong rides,
And lifts his horse, with bloody spurs deep buried
in his sides.

God's mercy! does he see the gulf? Ha! now his purpose dawns
Upon our minds, as nearer still the rocky fissure yawns:
Where from the farther side the stone leans o'er the stream beneath,
He means to take the awful leap! Cold horror checks our breath,
And still and mute we watch him now: he nears the fearful place;
We hear him shout to cheer the horse, and keep the headlong pace.
Then comes a rush, — short strides, — a blow! — the horse bounds wildly on,
Springs high in air o'er the abyss, and lands upon the stone!
It trembles, topples 'neath their weight! it sinks! ha! bravely done!
Another spring, — they gain the side, — the ponderous rock is gone
With crashing roar, a thousand feet, down to the flood below,

And Hilton, heedless of its noise, is riding at the
foe!

"The Frenchman stared in wonder: he was brave,
and would not run,
'Twould merit but a coward's brand to turn and
fly from one.
But still he shuddered at the glance from 'neath
that knitted brow:
He knew 'twould be a death fight, but there was
no shrinking now.
He pressed his horse to meet the shock: straight at
him Hilton made,
And as they closed the Frenchman's cut fell harm-
less on his blade;
But scarce a moment's time had passed ere, spur-
ring from the field,
A troop of cuirassiers closed round and called on
him to yield.
One glance of scorn he threw them, — all his answer
in a frown, —
And riding at their leader with one sweep he cut
him down;

Then aimed at him who held the flag a cut of
crushing might,
And split him to the very chin! — a horrid, ghastly
sight!
He seized the standard from his hand; but now
the Frenchmen close,
And that stout soldier, all alone, fights with a
hundred foes!
They cut and cursed, — a dozen swords were whis-
tling round his head;
He could not guard on every side, — from fifty
wounds he bled.
His sabre crashed through helm and blade, as
though it were a mace;
He cut their steel cuirasses and he slashed them
o'er the face.
One tall dragoon closed on him, but he wheeled
his horse around,
And cloven through the helmet went the trooper
to the ground.
But his sabre blade was broken by the fury of the
blow,

And he hurled the useless, bloody hilt against the
nearest foe ;
Then furled the colors round the pole, and, like a
levelled lance,
He charged with that red standard through the
bravest troops of France!
His horse, as lion-hearted, scarcely needed to be
urged,
And steed and rider bit the dust before him as he
charged.
Straight on he rode, and down they went, till he
had cleared the ranks,
Then once again he loosed the rein and struck his
horse's flanks.
A cheer broke from the French dragoons, — a loud,
admiring shout! —
As off he rode, and o'er him shook the tattered
colors out.
Still might they ride him down : they scorned to fire
or to pursue, —
Brave hearts! they cheered him to our lines, —
their army cheering, too!

And we — what did we do? you ask. Well, boy,
we did not cheer,
Nor not one sound of welcome reached our hero
comrade's ear;
But, as he rode along the ranks, each soldier's head
was bare, —
Our hearts were far too full for cheers, — we wel-
comed him with prayer.
Ah! boy, we loved that dear old flag, — ay, loved
it so, we cried
Like children, as we saw it wave in all its tattered
pride!
No, boy, no cheers to greet him, though he played
a noble part, —
We only prayed 'God bless him!' but that prayer
came from the heart.
He knew we loved him for it, — he could see it in
our tears, —
And such silent earnest love as that is better, boy,
than cheers.
Next day we fought the Frenchman, and we drove
him back, of course,

Though we lost some goodly soldiers, and old Picton lost a horse.
But there I 've said enough: your mother's warning finger shook, —
Mind, never be a soldier, boy! — now let me have a smoke."

www.ingramcontent.com/pod-product-compliance
Lightning Source LLC
LaVergne TN
LVHW050528100826
845148LV00002B/484

* 9 7 8 1 4 2 5 5 1 9 3 6 0 *